THE GREAT NUMBER RUMBLE

**Cora Lee &
Gillian O'Reilly**

Illustrations by Virginia Gray

annick press
toronto + new york + vancouver

Annick Press Ltd.

We acknowledge the support of the Canada Council for the Arts, the Ontario Arts Council, the Government of Canada through the Book Publishing Industry Development Program (BPIDP) for our publishing activities.

Edited by Pam Robertson
Copy edited by Derek Fairbridge
Proofread by Melissa Edwards
Interior design by Irvin Cheung
Cover design by Naomi MacDougall

Cataloguing in Publication
Lee, Cora
    The great number rumble : a story of math in surprising places / by Cora Lee and Gillian O'Reilly ; illustrations by Virginia Gray.

Includes index.
ISBN-13: 978-1-55451-032-0 (bound)
ISBN-10: 1-55451-032-5 (bound)
ISBN-13: 978-1-55451-031-3 (pbk.)
ISBN-10: 1-55451-031-7 (pbk.)

    1. Mathematics—Juvenile literature. I. O'Reilly, Gillian II. Gray, Virginia III. Title.

QA40.5.L47 2007   j510   C2006-904893-2

Published in the U.S.A. by
Annick Press (U.S.) Ltd.

Distributed in Canada by
Firefly Books Ltd.
66 Leek Crescent
Richmond Hill, ON
L4B 1H1

Distributed in the U.S.A. by
Firefly Books (U.S.) Inc.
P.O. Box 1338
Ellicott Station
Buffalo, NY 14205

Printed and bound in China

Visit our website at www.annickpress.com

For Jaime and her friends, mathematicians in the making, and for Peter. — CL

For my father, who appreciates both numbers and words and who made Möbius strips for all our birthday parties. — GO

Thanks to Nancy Rawlinson, Jim O'Reilly, Evan Lee, Stan Jang, Fion Mok, Loris Lesynski, and Alan and Ian Usher for their help at various points along the way. — CL and GO

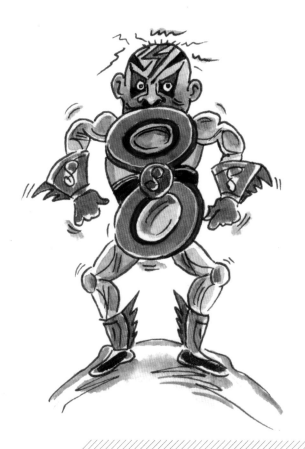

My friend Sam, he's crazy about math. Me (the name's Jeremy), I can do without it. Math has nothing to do with me, and I have nothing to do with it—except when it comes to homework, and then I'm the kind of guy who needs a calculator desperately. At least, that's what I thought until last fall, when we had our great math debate or, as I like to call it, "The Number Rumble." That was the day when…but wait, first let me tell you about Sam.

Sam was still new to the neighborhood when The Number Rumble happened. He had moved in next door a few weeks before school started. At first, I thought he was just like me: tall, dark, and good-looking, well, except that he's got red hair, and the light skin to go with it. And I don't wear glasses. And, okay, so the good-looking part's just an illusion. But we liked the same things, like swimming, blading, biking, video games. There was one major, *major* difference,

though—he was nuts about numbers and anything else to do with math. Not that he was studying all summer or anything. We goofed around a lot. Pretty soon, he was just Sam to me. A regular guy who saw the world differently—as numbers, shapes, and patterns.

What *is* math? Mathematics is making sense of amounts, shapes, and space. It's exploring how these kinds of things link up and fit together in patterns. It's way more than just numbers. So, what is math? The real question is: what isn't?

When we started school, everyone thought he was either a genius or a geek. Sam says he's neither. He prefers the word "mathnik"— thinks it describes us technology-crazy kids perfectly. No way, I said, not me. But Sam says we were all born mathniks. I wasn't so sure about that, but there's no arguing with the guy.

JEREMY WRESTLES WITH THE WEIRD STUFF:

Sam says that scientists can prove that babies recognize differences in the numbers of things— only two days after they're born! According to these scientists, then, as a baby I'd get bored seeing picture after picture showing two dots, no matter how the dots were arranged, but I'd get excited as soon as you switched to a picture of three dots. When I was a few months older I could tell the difference between bigger numbers like 8 and 16. At five months I'd get upset if you tried to show me that one toy plus one toy equals three, and at nine months, I knew that 5 + 5 = 10! Pretty smart back then, wasn't I? So what happened...?

Anyway, Sam's low-key about his talent—doesn't make a big deal about it. "Math is nothing special," he's always saying. "It's everywhere and in everything, and we all use it, not just me."

Well, one day, he had to prove it.

When the news first broke, there was cheering across the city. The director of education for our region had just announced that he was cutting math from the curriculum. No more math? Great, I thought. But when Sam's mom told him the news at breakfast, he said he jumped a mile—wait, Sam prefers metric, so make that 1.609 kilometers—out of his chair, like he was on fire. And he wasn't jumping for joy. He rushed straight upstairs to his computer to check out the details. Scanning the headlines, he clicked on "Goodbye Math: Kids Face Regional Math Ban":

Mathematics will be removed from the school curriculum, effective immediately, director of education Lawrence Lake announced today.

Lake says he has been considering the move for months, and believes that removing the topic will have little impact on students. "All kids need is a bit of basic arithmetic: addition, subtraction, multiplication and division," Lake said. "Heck, they can use calculators for most of that. Math isn't much more anyway. I mean, who needs the extra stress? Budgets bother me, statistics stump me, fractions frazzle me—if I'm having so much trouble with math, how's the average student or teacher going to get through it?"

Asked what parents and teachers thought, Lake cited widespread support for the move, saying many of them shared his views and were certain that children would experience less stress without mathematics.

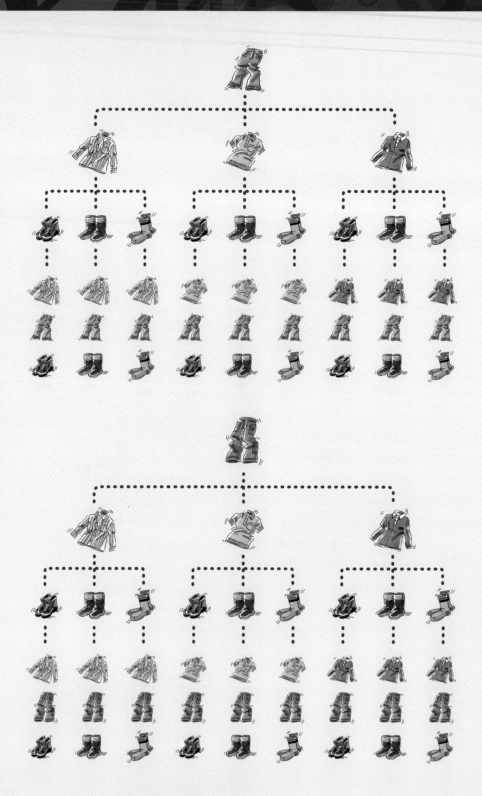

Sam told me he lost it then. He was so mad, he just threw on yesterday's clothes lying on the floor (hey, mathniks dump their clothes on the floor like the rest of us) and ran right over. That tells you how upset he was. Normally, he's the mix 'n' match master—he'd be consulting this big chart on his closet door for different combinations, never wearing the same thing twice.

Sam just about exploded through the door at my house. "Jeremy! Did you hear the news? No more math!"

"Sounds good to me," I responded immediately.

3 combinations

6 permutations

Most people have a favorite kind of ice cream. But mathniks like to look at *all* the options. First, the combinations: how many double-scoop cones can you get if the scoops are different flavors and it doesn't matter what flavor's on top? Then the permutations—how many if it *does* matter? (Permutations are for picky eaters!) Tip: if you're first in line looking at 198 flavors on a hot day—just choose chocolate!

"Are you kidding? No more fractions! No more percents! Geometry and graphs, gone. In all probability, no probability! How could they do this?"

He went on like this all the way to school. Half the time I couldn't figure out what he was talking about, but I could tell he needed to get it out of his system. Anyway, when we got there, it was a circus. Talk about chaos! Recycling bins full of math texts, notebooks, rulers, even calculators—and kids everywhere tossing in more! Teachers, too. I pointed out Mrs. Norton, our math teacher, to Sam—you should have seen the grin on her face. I always knew she hated teaching math.

The news cameras were there too.

JEREMY WRESTLES WITH THE WEIRD STUFF:

Sam's always getting on my case about the word "chaos." When I use it, I mean a huge, confused mess! But Sam says that in mathematics, chaos is something that's perfectly logical underneath, even though the situation is always changing and impossible to predict. That's because tiny changes at the start make a huge difference in the end. It's called the "butterfly effect." In weather systems, for example, the air stirred by a butterfly's wing can trigger other changes that lead, months down the road, to a hurricane halfway around the world! The same thing happens in pinball— the tiniest difference in the way you launch the ball changes its route in a major way.

Someone thrust a microphone in my face. "What do you think of the ban, kids? I guess you're pleased, eh?"

"I've got no problem with it," I said.

"Are you kidding?" Sam shoved me aside. "The idea is crazy! Does the director have any idea what life would be *like* without math? If I had just one afternoon with Mr. Lake, I'd show him just how much he needs it..."

"I think that's a great idea," cut in Ms. Kay, the school librarian, before the startled reporter could question Sam further. "Why don't we organize a little debate right here at our school? It would be an excellent learning opportunity...for young Samuel and Jeremy, and the other kids, of course."

She was smiling sweetly as she said this, but I wondered what she was planning. Ms. Kay had a way of getting people to do what she wanted, and the way she made out that Sam was some ordinary kid seemed...well, sneaky. And she's a teacher!

Anyway, the reporter whipped out her cell phone, called the director of education and asked if he would come to the school for "a little debate with a concerned student." He laughed and said sure, he'd come by during lunch. The reporter hung up and nodded at us. "See you back here at lunch then."

I glanced at Ms. Kay's face as we left. Why did she look so pleased?

Word got out about the debate. When Sam and I walked in at noon, the gym was almost full: there were news reporters, a TV crew, our teachers, the principal and vice principal, the director of education and his people, and more kids than I expected. Ms. Kay had set up a microphone and a couple of chairs for Sam and Mr. Lake.

"Hey Sam," I said. "I know *you* really like math, but there are a lot more people like me who don't think it's so interesting, and the director hates it. How are you going to convince him?"

"Don't worry," he answered, "I've got a plan."

Don't worry? I didn't exactly want his plan to work, whatever it was. Still, Sam's my friend, so maybe I didn't want him to look stupid up there. I followed him through the gym and grabbed a seat up front to watch the action.

Ms. Kay introduced the debaters and asked Mr. Lake to speak first. The director stepped up to the mike, smiling and nodding to the audience, like we were all his fans or something.

A number's a number, right? Wrong, says Sam. We've got natural numbers (1, 2, 3, and so on) and whole numbers, which are the natural numbers and zero (0, 1, 2, 3...)—hey, did you know that when Indian mathematicians first began using zero, the Europeans actually thought it was evil? How can you write nothing?, they thought. It was all wrong! Anyway, putting zero and negative numbers in with the positives gets you the set of integers (...-3, -2, -1, 0, 1, 2, 3...), which is useful on a thermometer, I guess.

Rational numbers are numbers you can write as decimals or fractions, which are ratios of two whole numbers (rational, ratios...get it?), like 1/2 or 4/3. Irrational numbers are things like the square root of two, written as √2 or 1.41421356..., and pi or π, which is 3.141592653... They're numbers you can't write as a fraction or as a decimal, because they just go on and on, never ending—or at least no one's found an end yet. And these numbers don't show any

logical repeating pattern either. Irrationals seemed so...well, *irrational*, that when the square root of 2 was discovered, it got a man killed (find out more at the end of this chapter). The ones I've already mentioned aren't the only types of numbers either, but when Sam started in on imaginary numbers, I said, "Whoa! Stop right there!" (But if *you* want to know more, check the glossary.) Why can't we be like the Pirahã tribe in Brazil, and just use *one, two* and *many*?!

"Well, well, well," he said to Sam. "I hear you have some concerns about my decision. What is it—you're going to miss irrational and imaginary numbers? Who needs them when we have enough trouble with real ones!" He looked around to see how we liked his little joke, his smile growing broader with every word. "Or is it word problems? I promise you, you won't need those. When was the last time anyone told you he was eight years younger than four times the square root of your sister's age?"

You could tell the director thought he was pretty clever. He went on: "Don't be afraid to speak up, son. I'm sure I can answer your questions and help you appreciate our point of view."

"I doubt it," said Sam, not smiling. "In fact, I'm so sure that you've made the wrong decision that I propose a kind of bet."

"A bet?" chuckled the director.

"Yes," said Sam. "I'm going to convince you and everyone here that math is not only important, but exciting too, and part of everything we do. And if I can't make you change your mind, I promise to work for you every day after school for the whole year."

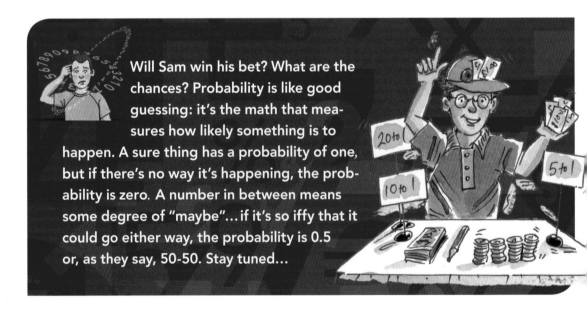

Will Sam win his bet? What are the chances? Probability is like good guessing: it's the math that measures how likely something is to happen. A sure thing has a probability of one, but if there's no way it's happening, the probability is zero. A number in between means some degree of "maybe"...if it's so iffy that it could go either way, the probability is 0.5 or, as they say, 50-50. Stay tuned...

"For free? Don't get too confident now," said the director.

I wasn't so keen on getting math back, but I didn't like that smirk on the director's face. Still, I couldn't believe the offer Sam was making. What was he up to?

"Well, no. I was going to suggest that you pay me one cent a day for the first day, then double it to two cents the second, four cents the third, eight cents the fourth, and so on."

"You certainly won't get rich that way," laughed the director. "But sure, it's a deal."

He settled back, smiling so widely I thought his face would split. I saw the vice principal open his mouth to say something, but then he closed it when he caught Ms. Kay's eye. She winked at him and he winked back. Something was definitely going on. I just couldn't figure out what it was.

"Alright, let's start right here in the gym," said Sam.

"Are you sure, son? Not much math here—"

Sam just looked him over calmly. "There's some right in front of you." Sam waved our class's super-athlete over. She had just returned to the school after a training ride for her next bike race. "Emily—come here a minute, would you?"

"Hey, Sam. Hello, Mr. Lake," she said, leaning her bike against the wall. "How am I supposed to help? I mean, math's okay, but it's got nothing to do with me."

"Sure it does," Sam said quickly. "Biking is geometry in motion."

And with that, the great debate was on.

"Almost all bike frames have triangles in them—that's the strongest shape there is," continued Sam. "The triangles won't collapse under the rider's weight, even with all the bumps, braking, and hard pedaling. It's the same reason you see triangles in bridges, skyscrapers, and geodesic domes."

"I wasn't sure about those fancy specialty bikes at first," continued Sam. "But the basic triangle's there—just curved or cut away so things like shocks can fit. Besides, newer metals like chromium and titanium are stronger than steel, so bike designers can experiment more."

"Hold on..." I couldn't help interrupting. I was picturing my own bike, and Sam's. "In my bike, the triangle is flatter than Emily's, and the one in yours is even flatter. Are they supposed to be different?"

"Those are clues to the kind of riding we're into," said Sam. "Yours is a mountain bike. Mountain bikes are made for off-road riding—barrelling through streams and jolting over rocks. You need to stay low to keep from tipping. That's why a mountain bike's back triangle is short and wide.

"Mine is a BMX—it's built to fly! A super-skinny back triangle brings me down even lower, really close to the ground. It's perfect for jumping, spinning, and flying around a track full of bumps, jumps, and berms. It makes it easier to pedal hard when I need more speed, too."

"And mine," said Emily, "doesn't have to be low to the ground because I don't need to twist, turn, or jump."

"Right," agreed Sam. "Road bikes are built for long, smooth rides or road races. Tipping isn't so much of a problem and you want to be comfortable while you pedal—that's what tall, thin triangles give you."

"Too bad that doesn't get me up hills any easier," I said, thinking about the trip home later. "I can gear all the way down and still can't make it to the top without stopping."

"That's geometry, too—circles this time, and their ratios," added Sam. "A ratio is just a way to compare two numbers. In this case, we're comparing the sizes of the front and back gears, which control how many times your wheel goes around each time you turn your pedals."

That whole pedal-gear-chain setup—it's inspired. Ever try riding uphill without gears? On a bike with gears, you can move the chain to hook up any pair of front and back gears you want, depending on how hard you want to work. A high gear ratio (big front gear, small back one) gets you more turns of the wheel each time you turn the pedal. It's perfect for riding on flat roads, when pushing hard to cover more ground is okay. Not like up a hill. Then, who cares about distance? Gear down quick for a low gear ratio (small front gear, big back gear) and sacrifice ground covered for easier riding. A cyclist might think it's just smart pedaling, but mathniks know better: the secret's in the ratios.

"But hold on, Sam," said Emily "I've seen gears that aren't circles—they're oval, like ellipses."

"True. My dad's bike has elliptical gears in the front and circles in the back. Wish I could have them on my own bike. Some cyclists think this shape gives each push more power. Others don't agree." Sam shrugged. "Doesn't matter to me. I just like the shape."

What did I tell you? Everything is a shape or a pattern to Sam. For him a bike was all triangles and circles—or ellipses.

Emily was fascinated—but she likes knowing how things work. The biking tips were great but I was glad I didn't actually have to do the math! Mr. Lake wasn't too impressed. "A bike is a bike," he said. "And getting up a hill takes simple, hard work—not thinking about a lot of numbers and shapes."

Sam was ready with another example. "It's not just in cycling," he said. "There's math in basketball, too. You can make more baskets by

What's a bike with square wheels? Useless —ha ha! But seriously, Sam told me about a mathematics professor named Stan Wagon who actually built a bike with square wheels! Of course, he had to build his own road, too. It had evenly spaced bumps of just the right size and shape, what he called "inverted catenaries." A catenary is the curve you get when you let a skipping rope or a chain hang with an end in each of your hands. Imagine a row of these upside down, and Professor Wagon's weird wheels rolling over it. Pentagonal (5-sided) wheels roll on inverted-catenary roads too, but the bumps have to be flatter and shorter in length. Hexagonal (6-sided) wheels need even smaller bumps. In fact, the more sides a wheel has, the flatter and shorter the bumps have to be. So what do you get if you keep on adding sides? You guessed it—a round wheel on a flat road!

simply adjusting the angle of your launch. And if angles aren't math, I don't know what is."

He walked over to pick up a basketball sitting at the side of the gym. "Anything you throw into the air goes up, then down, in a parabola shape. At first the ball travels both up and away, but then gravity wins out and the ball starts falling. How far it gets depends a lot on the angle you launch the ball at," explained Sam. "If you shoot at an angle that's too low—and nothing else about your shot changes—then gravity drags the ball down before it gets very far. If you launch high, it goes a long way up, but only a short way forward. Watch."

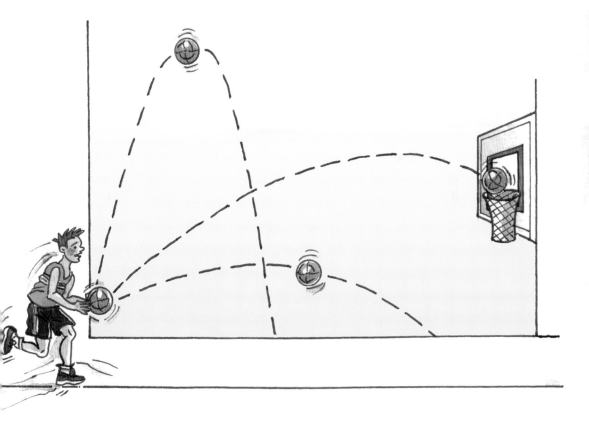

"Turns out," continued Sam, "that a medium angle—45 degrees—gets you the best distance, if that's what you want. That's pretty useful for punting a football, throwing a ball, javelin, or discus, or even winging a water balloon! And, from where I'm standing," he said, lobbing the ball into the basket with a swoosh, "it's also perfect for a basket."

I wondered what angle would get me and my skateboard flying the farthest. You won't hear complaints from me if I can skate for my next math project.

"That's all kind of cool," said Emily. Obviously, she agreed with Sam. Some of the other kids jumped up, grabbed more basketballs, and tried to perfect their free throws by shooting basketballs at low, medium, and high angles. For my part, I was still hoping it wouldn't convince Mr. Lake—though a skateboarding project would be fun. But who was I kidding? They'd never accept that as a math assignment.

The gym was pretty noisy for a minute, but the vice principal, who always carries a very loud whistle, brought us back to order quickly and asked Mr. Lake for his response.

"Sorry," he replied. "You'll have to do better than that if you're going to convince me that math is part of everything we do. There can't be too many kids in the area who are serious enough about sports to actually use the math."

"You know something?" said Sam with a grin, "Statistically speaking, you're right. The serious athletes are a small percentage of the whole, and a wider survey might better reflect the majority."

All is number. Pythagoras of Samos, Greece, couldn't have picked a more perfect, more cryptic motto for the semi-scientific, quasi-religious secret society known as the Order of Pythagoras. The mysterious Pythagoras practically became a god to his followers, although he started out by bribing his first student to listen. But the boy was hooked: he even offered to pay for lessons when Pythagoras pretended he'd run out of bribe money.

Pythagoras's followers wore the sacred pentagram, or five-pointed star. The rules of this secret society were strict and many—own nothing, live as a group, and eat no meat, for starters. But the goal was simple: find proof that the universe is based on whole numbers.

The Pythagoreans reached some bizarre conclusions—that numbers had personalities and genders, and that 10 was sacred. But other discoveries were brilliant: harmonious ratios, triangle numbers, square numbers, and the Pythagorean Theorem, which describes the relationship between sides of a right triangle ($a^2 + b^2 = c^2$).

Evidence for a mathematical universe was growing (or so the Pythagoreans thought). Then, disaster struck. A Pythagorean named Hippasus discovered the square root of two, which was impossible to write as a ratio of whole numbers. A cover-up ensued, then murder, as Hippasus betrayed his oath of secrecy and was drowned by fanatic Pythagoreans. After Pythagoras himself died, the Order weakened and eventually self-destructed.

Several kids giggled at the director's blank look. Hey, even I knew a thing or two about statistics. To put it another way: we can't let a small group like the serious sports nuts speak for the rest of us.

Mr. Lake frowned, then looked suspiciously at Sam. "Statistics? I'm sure I meant no such thing. All I'm saying is that we must keep things in perspective, look at the big picture."

I was surprised Sam didn't drag out more examples, like the math in baseball and hockey stats, and scorekeeping for almost any game— maybe he would have, but just then someone shouted.

"Did you say picture?"

It was Oscar. Uh-oh. This wasn't going to be good for Sam. Where Sam was numbers and logic, Oscar was all creativity and emotion. He was great at art, bad at math—and didn't care who knew it. "Better stay away if you want your math back, Sammy," Oscar said. "Art and math, they don't mix. Math is just numbers, it's got nothing to do with art."

"You'd be surprised," replied Sam, leading us out of the gym.

Oscar just sneered. "Maybe you're thinking preschool—that's where you just make pretty patterns," he said. "Real artists don't work like that."

Some of the kids laughed at what Oscar said, and I found myself joining them. Unfortunately Sam noticed. He stayed cool, though—except for the look he gave me—and motioned for us all to follow him into the art room. As we crowded in, Sam pointed to a couple of posters on the wall.

"Escher's a real artist, don't you think?" Sam asked.

"Who?" The question came from a few kids.

"M.C. Escher," said Oscar. "And, of course, he's a real artist—a great 20th-century graphic artist—that's *artist*, not mathematician," he emphasized.

"True," said Sam, unfazed. "Escher wasn't a mathematician. But check out his artwork: it's loaded with math. His pictures show impossible things. Sometimes, it's like he's drawn infinity—the scenes go on and on..."

"Like Oscar, when he's talking about himself," I offered. Sam laughed.

"A lot of those mind-bending illusions have tessellations in them," Sam continued. "Like this one with lizards moving endlessly in and out of the background." Sam pointed to one of the posters.

"And tessellations are…?" I prompted.

"Shapes that tessellate fit together perfectly with no gaps or overlaps," said Sam.

"Kind of like the game Tetris?" I asked.

"Kind of," Sam agreed. "Same basic idea. In Tetris, the shapes are called tetrominoes. You want to lock them together to fill up rows so there aren't any gaps."

"A soccer ball's a tessellation, then," added Emily, "and so is the tread on my sneakers. And tiles on the floor or counter, and around the tub."

Sam was nodding, but there was something I didn't understand. "But Escher's pictures look nothing like what you're describing," I protested.

"Well, most of these examples are pretty basic," said Sam. "The simplest tessellations are made from just one shape with the same size angles and sides all around, like triangles, or squares, or hexagons. Then you've got the ones made from two or more shapes."

"Hold on," interrupted Oscar. "This hasn't got anything to do with Escher! He did way more than just put shapes together."

"Sure, Oscar, but even his most complicated illusions started out as simple shapes," said Sam, looking toward the posters again.

"Impossible!" said Mr. Lake.

"I'll show you," said Sam, heading for the supply cupboard. He took out scissors, tape, two jars of paint, a piece of poster paper, and a bag of craft foam. Selecting a square piece of foam, he continued, "It's like this: when you create your basic tiling shape, you can take anything you like from one side as long as you put it back on the opposite side."

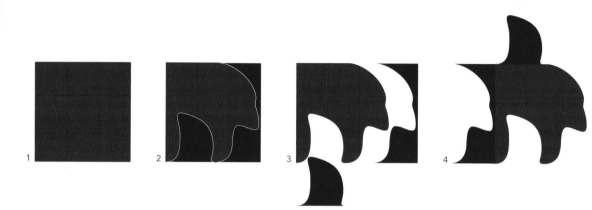

1 2 3 4

Sam cut a squiggly shape from one side of the square and taped it to the opposite side. He cut another shape from the bottom and taped it to the top.

"That's one weird shape," I said. "It's never going to tessellate."

"It will," said Sam. Tracing the finished shape onto another piece of foam, he cut out a copy and showed how the two pieces fit together on all sides. Then, taking the lids off the jars of paint, he dipped his foam shape into the red paint. Stamping his shape at the top left corner of the poster, he motioned for me to take the other copy and do one next to his with the green paint.

Taking turns, we quickly covered the paper with red and green figures, neatly side by side and down the page. Easy Escher! Not bad—to my eyes, at least.

"That's no Escher," said Oscar, barely looking at our masterpiece. "But, yeah, okay, I'll give you that point. But whatever. That's graphic art. I'm more into art that looks real, where math doesn't matter at all."

"Are you kidding? What about special effects? Some of the most

realistic stuff in movies is made using CGI," said Sam. "And then there's photography—but let's not go into that."

Oscar couldn't argue the point about special effects. The other kids were nodding too, and started tossing out their opinions on exactly which movie had the best CG effects. Mr. Lake shut down that debate. "Enough of that," he said in a loud voice. "Now, will somebody please tell me what CGI is?"

"That's computer generated imagery," Sam replied. "Digital animation. And computers run on math. Can I use this laptop?" He looked at the art teacher, who nodded his permission.

"I mean, you can build a totally fake world inside that screen. For each object,

you start with a frame—like a skeleton made up of small, connected shapes, sometimes thousands of them or the curves won't look real. So something like this CG dog gets stored as numbers and equations, all describing the corners, edges, and faces on each of a thousand shapes. Next, you drop a computer-generated, two-dimensional surface over the frame—it's like applying wallpaper or wrapping a present."

"Don't forget shading," said Oscar. "Shading is *crucial* for realism in art."

"Don't worry, Oscar," said Sam, rolling his eyes. "The computer has millions of colors for painting each pixel so that the shading's just right. Making a virtual world realistic is all tied in to lighting and shadow. Getting the lighting right takes tons of equations: one method, called 'ray tracing,' plots out the path that every imaginary ray of light would take from its source to its final landing place—including every bounce off imaginary mirrors and walls."

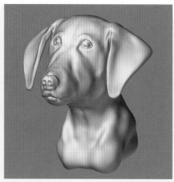

"Okay—your dog there looks pretty solid," admitted Oscar, "but aren't you forgetting something...you know, like fur?"

"We're getting there," replied Sam. "Hair is getting easier for CG artists to do, but it still takes a lot of data to capture the right shading, highlights, shape, curl, and even clumping, like with oily hair. For *The Lion, the Witch and the Wardrobe* movie, animators created seven different fur types, made up of 5.2 million digital hairs, to get Aslan looking like a real lion." Sam added hair to his dog. "Lucky for us, the school's software package makes it pretty easy to give this puppy a decent enough fur coat."

"That's not bad," said an older boy I didn't know. "CG people in old movies and games used to have hair like helmets!" He laughed. "The skin looked pretty pathetic, too."

"But not anymore. Remember Sunny, in the Lemony Snicket movie, *A Series of Unfortunate Events*? She had a digital double for some shots— you could hardly tell she wasn't a real baby. Even fantasy creatures look real—think about Dobby in *Harry Potter,* or Yoda in Episode II of *Star Wars,* or Gollum in *The Lord of the Rings,*" said Sam. "The software's getting so good you forget about the zillions of calculations that have to be processed just to get *one* of these guys on screen."

"Cool," said the older boy. "But there's almost never just one character or thing onscreen. What happens then?"

"Then, the computer has to calculate the size of one thing compared to another," answered Sam. "What's in front, what part's covered..."

"That's not even counting the actual animating part," I commented.

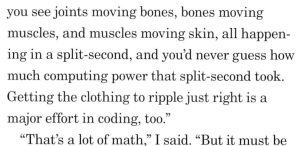

"Which takes more equations," said Sam, "because each time something spins, shifts, changes size, or even blinks, you need a new image. To get the illusion of moving characters, you need to see 30 to 60 images *each second*. The software's gotten so sophisticated that you see joints moving bones, bones moving muscles, and muscles moving skin, all happening in a split-second, and you'd never guess how much computing power that split-second took. Getting the clothing to ripple just right is a major effort in coding, too."

"That's a lot of math," I said. "But it must be easier doing crowds…there you can just kind of clone one thing over and over—can't you?"

"You'd think. But you can't, or you'll get a hokey army of clones," answered Sam. "What animators do is set up a few basic models with mix-and-match heads, bodies, clothes, and so on for variety in looks. Some movements can be copied from one to another, but to get every individual in a crowd acting just a bit differently, the computer needs certain mathematical rules. If this crowd is also going somewhere, the computer instructs each character to move with its neighbors in the same general direction, and not to go crashing into each other."

"I don't know. It's pretty cool…but that's a lot of math," said Oscar.

"Nobody expects you to do the math—unless you're the one creating the software," said Sam.

It's a good thing somebody invented computers. Look at the numbers it took to get these movies done! *The Lord of the Rings: The Return of the King* needed 3,200 computer processors running 24 hours a day and a team of 430 digital effects specialists to develop almost 600,000 Orcs, roughly 6,000 Rohan horsemen, and other fantastic creatures. *Shrek*'s got 68 characters and has all the tough stuff, like hair, fur, cloth, fire, fluids, and crowds. It took 60,406 polygons to build just one of the ordinary characters. There are 28,186 trees with three billion leaves, and 700 shots with moving cloth. The movie took a team of 275 animators and technical directors three years to finish. It's the fifth all-digital, feature-length animated movie ever made.

Toy Story was the first. It had 76 characters and 366 objects to put onscreen. All this took 4.5 million lines of code, involved 500,000 basic arithmetic operations per pixel, and 28 animators and 30 technical directors.

"But even as the artists, you *are* depending on math to make it easy for you."

"Yeah, I guess," said Oscar, "but we can always go back to pen and paper." He held up his sketchpad and a pencil. "This is all I need to draw portraits, landscapes, and comics. In fact, I kind of like manga—Japanese-style comics—right now. And a bonus: no math required."

"Any kind of drawing, even comics, uses math," said Sam. He pulled forward the flip chart standing at the side of the art teacher's desk. "Think about it. It's a 3-D world, but the paper you draw on is only 2-D.

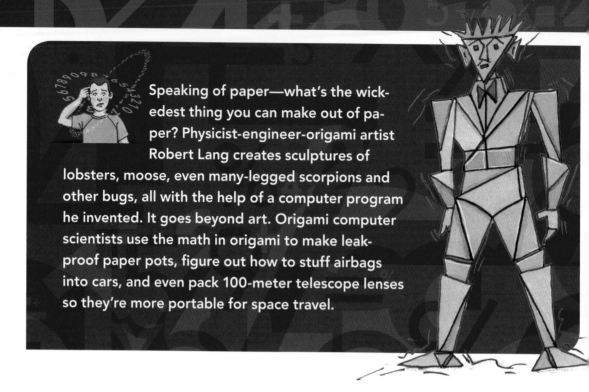

Speaking of paper—what's the wickedest thing you can make out of paper? Physicist-engineer-origami artist Robert Lang creates sculptures of lobsters, moose, even many-legged scorpions and other bugs, all with the help of a computer program he invented. It goes beyond art. Origami computer scientists use the math in origami to make leakproof paper pots, figure out how to stuff airbags into cars, and even pack 100-meter telescope lenses so they're more portable for space travel.

So how do you get from this," Sam said, scribbling a diamond on the flip chart, "to this?" He pointed to a carefully sketched amd shaded picture of a diamond tacked to the wall near the Escher prints.

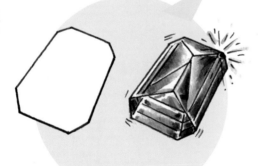

"That's perspective," said Oscar. "Not math."

"Back in the 15th century," explained Sam, "the Renaissance artists—who were also mathematicians, scientists, and musicians—started noticing that things seemed to change size and shape depending on where you stood. So they did all the math—"

"You're not listening," persisted Oscar. "All you need to know is perspective!"

"—and then they translated that into the

Archimedes is one of the greatest mathematical geniuses ever. But an old manuscript says he's even smarter than anybody thought!

The multi-talented Greek mathematician made discoveries about pi, the volumes and surface areas of spheres and cylinders, and got us all saying "Eureka!" whenever a brilliant idea hit. The sight of water overflowing from the tub as he got into his bath sparked the solution to a tricky problem. Jumping right out of the tub, Archimedes sped naked through Syracuse, his hometown in Italy, shouting *"Eureka!"* (I've found it!). His many inventions included weapons of war—very handy against the Romans, who were invading Syracuse. His ideas were so valuable that, when Syracuse was finally captured, a Roman general gave orders to keep Archimedes alive. Sadly, it was his love of math that got Archimedes killed—an impatient soldier ran a sword through the old man when he refused to follow until he was done solving his geometry problem!

Scribes copied Archimedes' ideas for centuries but eventually the goat-skin pages of the last copy were scraped and recycled into a prayer book. Starting in 1998, scientists used digital enhancement, x-ray fluorescence, and imaging techniques to read Archimedes' words under the prayers. They discovered that the ancient genius understood infinity and even calculus—a math supposedly invented almost 2,000 years after his death, and used every day by modern scientists and engineers.

system of clues called perspective, which is what you use to do all your comics and other drawings," finished Sam.

Oscar turned bright red. *Ha!* Now Sam started drawing.

"See? You make circular things look oval if they're supposed to be seen from an angle. And when you draw a road leading off into the distance, you have to make the sides of the road meet at a point called the 'vanishing point,' even though they'd never touch in real life."

He handed the marker to Oscar. "Draw us a scene from one of your comics," said Sam. "Manga, superheroes, whatever. We can check for vanishing points and see if your geometry checks out."

I don't think Oscar was too keen on the idea, but he took the marker and sketched out a quick scene of a man tied to train tracks. When he finished, Sam picked up a red marker and ruler, and got to work finding parallel lines and drawing them out until they connected.

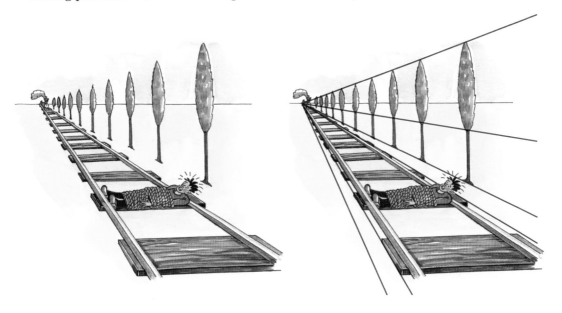

"There—not bad!" said Sam. "Looks like you're a mathematician after all."

Now, Sam's a smart guy. But sometimes, he just doesn't get it, especially where people are concerned. And telling Oscar he was a mathematician…well, that was definitely a mistake.

"An artist's genius and a mathematician's mind!" Oscar was admiring his own work. "No wonder I'm so good!"

See what I mean? Luckily, Oscar's show-off session was cut short by Jen. "Don't think you're the only artist-mathematician here," she said, rolling her eyes. "There's plenty of math in music."

"Huh?" said Oscar.

Jen's crazy about music—Jen and her friends even have their own band—but she likes math, too. And Sam can play a mean keyboard, when he puts his mind to it. So when she and Sam get going, watch out! It's like math and music rule the universe.

"Music and math *belong* together!" Jen continued. "Your Renaissance artists knew it. Even people back in the Middle Ages knew it! I can't believe you don't see the connection." She got so intense that Oscar started backing away. "The four classes you absolutely had to take in medieval universities were arithmetic, geometry, astronomy, and *music*." Jen turned to confront Mr. Lake. "That's what *we* should do. Instead of taking away math, you should be putting in more music!"

Mr. Lake looked around helplessly.

"A lot of the Renaissance mathematicians were trained musicians, too," added Sam. "It's easy to see why."

"It is?" Mr. Lake squeaked out the question.

"Of course it is," said an exasperated Jen. "Come on…" She led Mr. Lake, Sam, and everyone else across the hall to the music room and grabbed the first sheet of music she saw from its stand. She pulled a sheet of her own music from her bag and thrust both into Mr. Lake's hands. "Just look at any piece of music. There's math all over it! The time signature even looks like a fraction. And the notes…their names are like fractions: whole note, half note, quarter note, eighth note, sixteenth note…"

"They add up like fractions, too: a half note and two quarter notes add up to one bar when the time signature calls for 4/4 time," added Sam. "But obviously there's way more math in music than just time signatures."

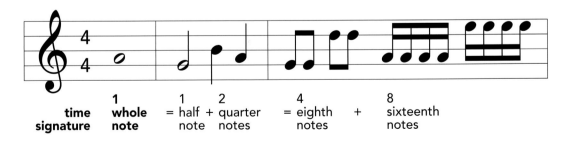

"I don't see…" began Mr. Lake.

Jen jabbed the paper impatiently. "Patterns! Patterns everywhere! It doesn't matter whether it's classical music or the latest rock song. See this small group of notes? It's called a 'motif' and it's repeated all over the place. When I write my own songs, I sometimes move the motif up, sometimes down, sometimes backwards, even upside down!"

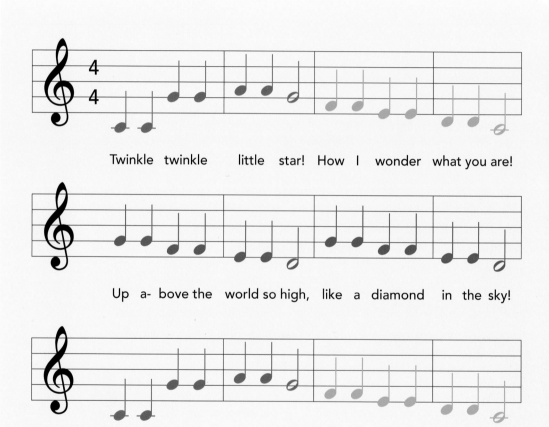

Twinkle twinkle   little   star! How I   wonder what you are!

Up a- bove the   world so high,   like   a   diamond   in the sky!

Twinkle twinkle   little   star! How I   wonder what you are!

Hypatia was as close to perfect as anyone could be. Her father, the mathematician Theon, wanted to create the ideal human being, so he made sure that Hypatia grew up healthy and educated. It worked—she became the greatest mathematician and astronomer of her time and an important public speaker and philosopher. She was also a popular teacher at the university at Alexandria in Egypt, which was famous for its huge libraries. And, legend says, Hypatia was so beautiful that she taught from behind a screen so she wouldn't distract her students! It was the wrong time and place to be so brilliant, though. Legitimate astronomers and mathematicians were getting a bad name because con artists were scamming the public with fake predictions. The Christians, who were fighting non-Christian philosophies and religions, were suspicious of Hypatia's speeches on philosophy. Hypatia's political friendships got her into trouble, too. A mob of fanatical monks attacked Hypatia on her way home one night. They dragged her to a church, hacked her to pieces and burned her remains. Some historians call this the start of the Dark Ages for Europe, when institutions such as the library at Alexandria were also destroyed. After this, Greek and Roman knowledge disappeared for 1,000 years.

"All those scales we practice, they follow a pattern, too," Jen went on. "And there's a pattern to what notes sound good together—like these two," she said, turning and playing middle C and high C together on the piano. "It's the same no matter what scale you're playing."

"Pythagoras noticed exactly the same thing centuries ago," Sam said. "He described it as a ratio of string lengths on his monochord—that's an instrument like a guitar but with only one string and a moveable bridge that slides along it. Pythagoras discovered that when he divided the string in half, the note he got was twice as high—that's

a ratio of two to one—as the note he got when he played the whole string."

"Let's try it out," I said, picking up the guitar I spied in the corner. "This first string is E. If you count down about halfway, this should be an E that sounds twice as high."

I gave my best imitation of Pythagoras as a rock musician with those two notes.

"Right," said Jen dryly, taking the guitar away from me. "Pressing down on different frets cuts the string into different lengths for other notes." She demonstrated a scale.

"Some other notes sound great together, too, like C and F, or C and G," continued Jen. "You find C and G together a lot, like in the opening notes of the *Star Wars* theme. When Pythagoras compared the lengths of the strings for C and G, he saw that the string for C was 3/2 longer than the string for G. When he looked at C and F, the string for C was 4/3 longer than the string for F. This was major news—"

How can musical ratios rule the world? Well, the numbers in those ratios—one, two, three, and four—were the same small whole numbers that the Pythagoreans were so nuts about already! It was like evidence for their version of the universe, which had the perfectly spherical sun, earth, and other planets moving in precise circles around each other, separated by harmonic ratios of their distances. Basically, they believed that the planets swished around each other, singing in perfect harmony!

It was? She was losing me—and it must have shown on my face, because Jen gave me this look, like it ought to be obvious. "*You* might not be impressed, but to Pythagoras, it was proof that ratios of small, whole numbers like two, three, and four ruled the world."

"That's all well and good for any of you taking music lessons," interrupted Mr. Lake. "But still hardly necessary. I myself never had music lessons, and I don't think too many of us are destined to become composers!"

The man had a point. Composing our own music? I was thinking Sam was stuck this time—but I was wrong. Leave it to the math master!

"Not true," said Sam. "Anybody can be a composer, especially now, if

Okay, so you don't play an instrument and you're not exactly keen on composing. But you do like your tunes, don't you? Your MP3 player squeezes a hefty 32-megabyte song down to a mere three megabytes by mathematically stripping out parts of the sound signal you don't need or can't hear, and replacing extra long or duplicate bits with shorter code. The results from this mathematical modification: near CD-quality music, downloadable in minutes, not hours!

you have a MIDI-equipped keyboard like mine. I can compose music in a ton of different instrument voices, program a backup band to play along with, and experiment with different tempos and effects. It records and prints out my music for me, too."

"It's great for our band," Jen put in.

"And the math?" asked Mr. Lake, frowning.

"It's there," replied Sam. "The keyboard understands only MIDI numbers—"

"Musical instrument digital interface numbers," supplied Jen, seeing the puzzled look on Mr. Lake's face. "Developed in 1983."

"Thanks," said Sam. "So, each time you press a key, you're putting musical instructions into code. One number is the note you're playing, another says how loud or how long, and another records which instrument voice you've chosen. So it's not music being recorded, it's math. Then, when you play back a recording, the numbers are decoded and turned back into sounds, which are already built into the keyboard."

"You know," cut in Jen, "this all sounds so high-tech, but using math to make music is nothing new. And the guys doing it 200 years ago didn't need computers either, just a pair of dice and a some scissors. Back in 1775, a manual with the longest title was produced. It was called," she took a deep breath, "*A Tabular System Whereby the Art of Composing Minuets is Made So Easy That Any Person, without the Least Knowledge of Musick, May Compose Ten Thousand, All Different, and in the Most Pleasing and Correct Manner.*"

"*Composing for Dummies* would be easier to remember," I said.

Jen went on, completely ignoring me. "All the 'composer' had to do was number the bars on a sheet of music written by someone else, cut them out, and rearrange them randomly—"

"Kind of like the sampling they do in hip-hop, only with Mozart or some other famous composer," added Sam.

"Except that hip-hop artists choose what they use," Jen explained. "And in the 1700s they used dice or other random-number generators to arrange the bits."

"The slice-and-dice method?" I offered. Now Sam *and* Jen were ignoring me, though I did get some snickers from the other kids.

"It was a sneaky move," said Sam. "Probability theory was still pretty new, but these guys knew the chances of rolling dice to get the exact same pattern of pieces were really, really low. So they could always count on rolling out an 'original' with this method."

"It *all* sounds a little too much like cheating…using math to help you do better in sports, art, and now music," said Mr. Lake. "I've never heard of such a thing and cannot allow it!"

"And I would have to agree with you, Mr. Lake." Mrs. Norton, the math-hating teacher, had been watching nervously. Now she rushed to speak up.

"**D**efinitely cheating.** Students should be working with their *natural* skills," continued Mrs. Norton. "You can't improve on nature, I always say—and nature can't be reduced to mathematical formulas!"

"That's not exactly true," said Sam. "There's more math out there than you think."

"If it's out there, can we get out there too?" asked a cameraman. "It's getting a little stuffy with all you people crowded in here."

"Why don't we go out to the new teaching garden by the science room?" suggested the vice principal. So we all trooped out there among the sunflowers and the butterfly-attracting plants and all the other stuff the science teacher made us plant last spring.

You'd think the garden would have a calming effect—I know I was always falling asleep in science class—but the bees were making Mrs. Norton even more nervous than usual. Or maybe just grouchier.

"Ridiculous. Look around you! Where can you possibly find math out here?" she snapped.

"Try right under your nose," said Sam in a deadpan voice, watching as a bee zoomed out of a flower directly in front of her.

Mrs. Norton gave a little shriek, and backed up, a little too close to an anthill. Another shriek. "Or your feet," added Sam, trying not to laugh.

"Get serious," I said. "Bees and ants?"

"That's what I said, when my mom's friend told me," said Sam. "She's a scientist studying these ants called Tunisian desert ants. These ants will zigzag all over the place searching for food. But as soon as they find something, they'll grab it and head straight back for the nest, like they've calculated a direct route."

"Humph. Probably following some trail—a smell, or chemical they've left behind," said Mrs. Norton.

"Except they can't be, or they'd go back following the zigzags of the path they took there. My mom's friend says it's 'dead reckoning'—that's how sailors and pilots used to navigate, long before the Global Positioning System was invented. In the 1960s and '70s, *Apollo* astronauts used dead reckoning on their moon missions. With dead reckoning, you can estimate where you should end up as long as you have accurate measurements."

"But Sam," Ms. Kay interjected. "Dead reckoning requires arithmetic and trigonometry, and the ability to measure speed, time, and direction. Ants don't have measuring instruments, nor do they have calculators."

Hmm. I thought she was on Sam's side. Or was Ms. Kay trying to get Sam to explain some more about this? Very sneaky…almost as sneaky as the way she set up this whole debate.

"The ants measure distance by counting their steps, and somehow they use the sun as a compass," said Sam. "The calculation's done totally by instinct. It's like their brains evolved so they can compute exactly what they need, automatically. They don't need to think through the procedure step by step, the way we do," began Sam.

"Good thing. If they had to, they might never get home," I joked.

"Other insects have their own ways of measuring things," said Sam. "That bee over there," he continued, directing everyone's attention to a bee headed for our observation hive in the corner, "estimates distance by processing how quickly images of trees and other markers move in its eyes as it flies past. It'll need this info when it gets back into the hive."

We made our way to the glassed-in hive. "Oh no," I exclaimed in spite of myself. "There's a tessellation in that honeycomb." I groaned. Sam had just succeeded in making me—math-avoiding me—see math.

Sam just grinned. "Sure, why not? Honeybees use wall-to-wall hexagons to make storage cells for honey. It's a smart choice. Triangles and squares tessellate by themselves too, but honeycombs made of tessellating hexagons hold more honey and take less wax to build. Less work, too."

Sam waited as the bee flew in through the plastic entry tube. "Here it is," he said, pointing to the bee inside. "Let's see how far it's come."

"It's probably flown a marathon—and won," laughed a reporter. "Looks like a victory dance it's doing."

"You could call it that," Sam replied. "The distance the bee's flown is coded into the 'dance,' which gives the other bees all the info they need to find the food source."

Mr. Lake looked doubtful. "It's just circling."

Circle Dance

"That means the food is close by—30 feet or less. If the bees need to go far, the dance gets more complicated," replied Sam.

Almost as though Sam had planned it, another bee swooped in through the plastic entry tube.

"See how this one dances in a figure-8 pattern? That part, up the middle, tells how far; the more time the bee spends waggling its body,

Figure-8 Dance

angle

angle showing direction of food compared to position of sun

waggle part of dance
1 second spent waggling =
1 km of distance between hive and food

the farther away the food is located," Sam explained. "The direction, too. The waggle up the middle is angled to show where the food is, compared to the sun's position."

"You're telling us that this little honeybee can measure distance, time, angles, and do all the calculations needed to plot out a course for other bees to follow?" Mrs. Norton was having a hard time with this. Mr. Lake, too.

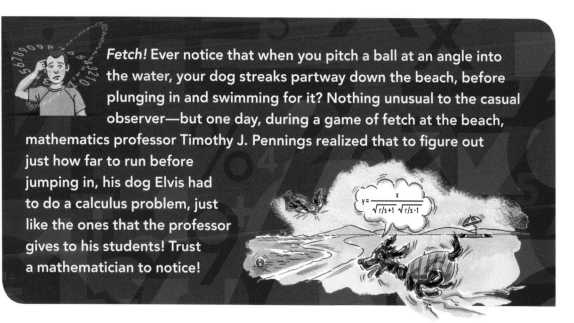

Fetch! Ever notice that when you pitch a ball at an angle into the water, your dog streaks partway down the beach, before plunging in and swimming for it? Nothing unusual to the casual observer—but one day, during a game of fetch at the beach, mathematics professor Timothy J. Pennings realized that to figure out just how far to run before jumping in, his dog Elvis had to do a calculus problem, just like the ones that the professor gives to his students! Trust a mathematician to notice!

$$y = \frac{x}{\sqrt{r/s+1}\ \sqrt{r/s-1}}$$

Sam shrugged. He was looking kind of discouraged at the stubborn looks on the teachers' faces. "Call it evolution, or instinct, if you want. It's not math the way we do math."

The next minute Sam looked at me and grinned. "I guess it's hard to take, the idea of a bug being smarter than you are," he whispered. Out loud, he said, "Maybe we should look at something that doesn't involve calculations. Math that's just there."

So if a lot of this stuff is instinct, can any animal do math like we can? I don't mean badly (ha ha!) but you know, can animals work with actual numbers, or at least with ideas like "more" or "less"? Well, Sam says that chimpanzee math comes the closest to ours: they understand fractions, can learn symbols for numbers, and can do easy adding and subtracting—kind of like your typical first grader. Then come the animals who do math like your baby brother: trained rats estimate well enough to get treats by pressing a lever the right number of times. And lions "count" the number of roars they hear before deciding whether they should stand and fight, or just run! And, shown two test tubes holding fruit flies (yum!), salamanders will choose the one holding more.

Mrs. Norton picked up a shiny, spiral-shaped shell decorating one of the flowerbeds. "Look at the beauty of this shell," she exclaimed. "You can't tell me this has anything to do with math."

"This shell," he said, "is a great example."

Mrs. Norton didn't look too pleased.

"It comes from a mollusk called the chambered nautilus. The animal starts out in a chamber smaller than a pea. But as it grows, the animal has to move outward, so it keeps building new shell chambers to fit a larger and larger body. The cool thing is," said Sam, tracing the spiral shape for us with his finger, "that it keeps the same angle as it winds outward, and ends up in a mathematical shape called a 'logarithmic spiral.'"

"What's so special about logarithmic spirals?" I asked.

"Got a piece of paper?" Sam asked, pulling out a pencil and a ruler. I handed him a couple of sheets—my math homework, actually. Sam put the shell on one sheet and drew a rectangle around it.

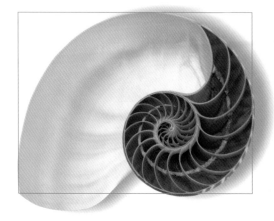

"This is a 'golden rectangle'—if you measure the sides and take their ratio, you get a number called the 'golden ratio,' also known as phi, or 1.618…" said Sam. "It's an irrational number—remember those? They're the ones that never end."

"And look," Sam continued, moving the shell off the paper, "if I divide this rectangle to get a square, the remaining rectangle is another golden rectangle. Keep doing this, and you get a smaller golden rectangle, and another, and another—you get the picture—and pretty soon you'll see a logarithmic spiral—the same spiral in the shell."

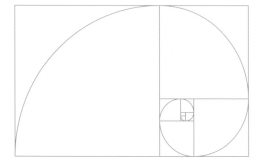

"More math in art," said Oscar importantly. "Leonardo da Vinci and other Renaissance artists thought golden rectangles—and other "golden" shapes—ruled. People say golden shapes show up in a lot of the Renaissance art and buildings. The artist in me never thought of it as math, but the mathematician in me sees it now."

Sam bent down to show us a growing plant. "Here's logarithmic spiraling again. The leaves spiral up this stem as they grow so that each leaf is perfectly positioned to get maximum sunlight. And look— there goes another example!" Sam stood up suddenly, pointing to the sky. I could just make out the shape of a peregrine falcon spiraling downward.

"It's after something!" I exclaimed. "Cool! But why doesn't it go straight down?"

"It's actually faster spiraling down," said Sam, shielding his eyes from the sun. A falcon's eyes are fixed to either side of its head. If it dives straight down, it's got to turn its head sideways to keep looking—that's not very aerodynamic so it slows the falcon down. Diving in a logarithmic spiral lets the falcon hold its head straight and still keep one eye on whatever it's chasing."

"On the Internet I saw a satellite photo of Hurricane Katrina over the Gulf of Mexico," said one kid. "That was a spiral, wasn't it?"

Hurricane Katrina
1445 UTC 29 August 2005
GOES-12 visible channel
over a MODIS true-color background

GOES Project NASA-GSFC

"You bet. And galaxies, too," said Sam, "like the Milky Way."

"Stop!" cried Mr. Lake. "Enough with the spirals! They're making me dizzy...I think I'm seeing spirals in the sunflowers!"

"That's because you *are* seeing them in the sunflowers," said Sam with a grin. "There are two groups of spirals in the middle of the sunflower, one winding clockwise and the other turning counter-clockwise. The number of spirals in each direction is a perfect example of 'Fibonacci numbers.'"

"And what," asked Mr. Lake in a tired, tired voice, "are Fibonacci numbers? Or do I want to know?"

"They're numbers that follow a particular pattern discovered by Fibonacci, the mathematician who brought the idea of zero to Europe. The sequence goes 1, 1, 2, 3, 5, 8, 13, and so on. Each new number comes from adding the two before."

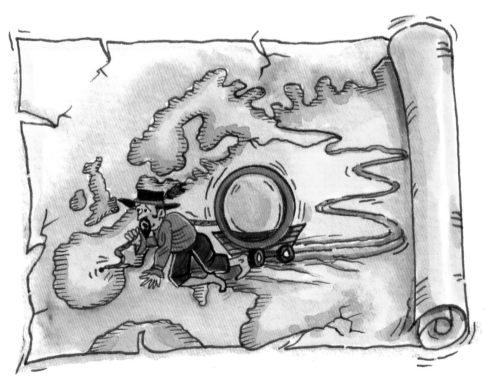

Fibonacci frenzy! Everywhere you go, Fibonacci numbers keep turning up in nature. The number of petals on some flowers, the number of spirals formed by the scales on a pineapple or the seeds in a sunflower, the number of seed chambers in an apple or a cucumber—they're all Fibonacci numbers. You'll even find them on your dinner plate. Next time you're served cauliflower, say you can't eat it because you have to count all the florets spiraling out from the center—it's your math homework!

At this point, Sam stopped and looked at Mr. Lake. "But you're right—time for a change."

Was that actually concern I was seeing on Sam's face? I took a look at Mr. Lake for myself—he *was* a little green. Maybe that's why Sam didn't go on about the Fibonacci numbers

As it turned out, Sam wasn't so concerned with Mr. Lake's condition. He was just eager to get on to something even more mind-bending. "Now for the really wild stuff!" said Sam.

Sam walked over to the window and asked the science teacher,

Ms. Oliva, for a laptop with Internet access. "Fractals!" he said, setting the computer up on a flat rock near a bunch of ferns growing under a tree. "The word 'fractal' comes from Latin, and means 'fractured'—you know, broken." Mr. Lake was mouthing the word at Mrs. Norton, who just shrugged helplessly. "See how each frond on this fern is made up of more fronds? Or look up: the branches of this tree look like smaller trees."

JEREMY WRESTLES WITH THE WEIRD STUFF!

Here's something really weird: these Fibonacci numbers are linked to those logarithmic spirals we talked about earlier. Check this out. Go along the Fibonacci sequence and divide each number by the one before it, like this: 2/1 = 2, 3/2 = 1.5, 5/3 = 1.667, 8/5 = 1.6, 13/8 = 1.625. Keep going—the answers get closer and closer to the irrational number 1.618...Spooky...

"I get it," said Emily. "Mountain ranges, too, with smaller and smaller jagged peaks, right down to the rocks. Or rivers, the way big ones split into small ones."

"A fractal is the same shape getting smaller and smaller?" I asked.

"Yup. Right into infinity...it's called 'self-similarity,'" answered Sam.

"That's nonsense—a branch can't go on forever," protested Mr. Lake.

"Not in real life," said Sam. "But fractals can go on and on in math—it's one of the coolest things about them."

"A parallel universe?" I suggested, not very seriously.

"You've been reading too many comics," Sam said. Then he turned serious. "It sounds like *Twilight Zone* stuff: fractal shapes aren't quite 1-, 2-, or 3-D. Think about it this way. You'd probably describe bread as a three-dimensional object. But it's not, really, because a 3-D object is solid, while bread's got lots of holes in it. Bread's definitely not 2-D, though, so it must be something in between—a fractional dimension between the second and third," said Sam. "Don't worry about the bread," Sam hurried to add, seeing Mr. Lake's totally bewildered face. That's just an example of something ordinary with fractional dimensions. Anyway, fractals have dimensions like 1.2 or 2.6. Another strange thing about fractals is that they can have infinite length, even if their areas are fixed."

"Bizarre," someone commented. "But if tree branches and ferns don't go on to infinity and fractals do, then what does a real fractal look like?"

"I'll show you some examples," said Sam, tilting the laptop screen so we could see."

"They're certainly very, uh, striking," said Mrs. Norton, "but I don't see the point of learning something that's just a curiosity."

"But they're not! You'd be amazed at what you can do with them," answered Sam. "Study population growth, analyze crystals, design cell-phone antennas, fight wildfires, clean up oil spills, and predict weather, earthquakes, and changes in the stock market...just to name a few!" Sam had to stop for a breath. "But remember we were talking about computer graphics? My dad showed me some old movies—"

"I can relate...my parents make me watch those, too," said Jen.

Sam went on: "The backgrounds looked so fake! I mean, compare those to our movies. Remember the bridge scene in *Fantastic Four,* when they show their superpowers for the first time? Fractals

Sophie Germain's parents were shocked: their 13-year-old daughter insisted on studying mathematics! Desperate, they took away her heat, candles, and clothes so she wouldn't study at night. It didn't work.

Why the fuss? Back in 18th-century Paris, serious math was for men. Sophie had it tough—no mathematician friends, tutors who wouldn't take her seriously, and a ban on women at the new math and science academy, L'École Polytechnique! So she sneaked lecture notes and submitted assignments as "Monsieur LeBlanc." But then her teacher —a famous mathematician named Legrange—wanted to meet the brilliant M. LeBlanc. Her secret was out: he was a she!

Germain hid behind her alter ego again when she started writing to the great German mathematician Carl Gauss. Did she blow her cover this time? You bet! When the emperor Napoleon's armies invaded Germany, she asked her friend, a French general, to make sure the great mathematician wasn't killed.

The general slipped up, and revealed her name. Gauss was shocked, but admired her brilliance and determination. Who wouldn't? Today, a school, a hotel, a street in Paris, and a certain set of prime numbers are named after Sophie Germain—not "Monsieur LeBlanc"!

were used to add depth to the water. And even the first fractal backgrounds, back in the 1980s, were amazing—like the planet Genesis in *Star Trek II: The Wrath of Khan*, or the Endor moon and the Death Star in *Return of the Jedi*. There's no way a computer can create images like these by modeling with smooth objects like spheres or cones, or even with frames made up of thousands more shapes than we used to make our CG dog. The only way to get infinite detail is to use infinite shapes like fractals."

"It all sounds a little…complicated," Mrs. Norton managed to say.

"Only when you need it to be—and a computer does all the real work," returned Sam. "The shapes may look complicated, but they all come from recycling results back into the same equation or rule—it's called 'iteration.'"

Sam picked up his pencil and another piece of paper. "Look, I can show you how easy it is to make a fractal called a 'Pythagorean tree': start with a rectangle and a triangle," he said, drawing as he spoke.

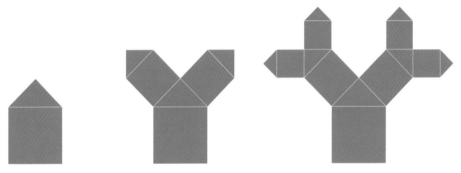

"The rule is: add another rectangle and triangle to each side of the triangle. The computer just keeps repeating that rule until it gets a tree, like this." He put aside his drawing and searched the Internet until he found the image he wanted.

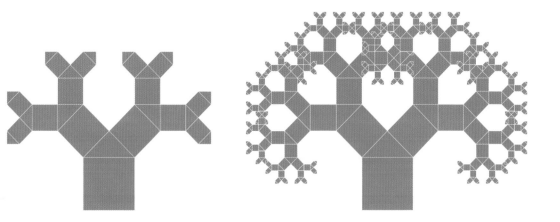

"That's basically what happens when CG moviemakers use fractals called L-systems to 'grow' natural stuff. L-system fractals make great plants and trees, even hair. So while fractals sound like science fiction, they're great tools for CG movie-makers," finished Sam.

"Hey, guys—lighten up," said Ralph. "Don't take all those special effects apart—you're draining all the magic out of them. I'll take my entertainment without the math. Too much work. I just want to have fun."

Consider this a warning: Ralph is unlike any other kid in school. Really. He once took an after-school comedy class, and the only comment the instructor gave was: "Ralph has his own brand of humor." Right. And that brand is "corny." For his birthday, instead of just having some kids over to eat pizza and watch DVDs, Ralph puts on his own show. We all like Ralph, but the problem is, his shows are always the same and all his jokes are real groaners.

"The words *fun* and *math* don't exactly go together," said Ralph.

"Why not?" asked Sam. "Math can be fun, even funny."

"Are you for real?" asked one kid. I think he spoke for everybody.

"What did one math book say to the other?" asked Sam.

"Huh?"

"What did one math book say to the other," he repeated patiently.

Hey, it doesn't matter if you win or lose—it's how you play the game. But I've been thinking —maybe Sam's got an unfair edge. He's more logical than I am (and has way more patience) when it comes to thinking through the permutations in puzzles like a Rubik's Cube. And he always wins at strategy games like checkers and chess. If I knew as much about probability as he does, I'd clean up in games of chance, too, like craps, roulette, or poker—not that we ever play those kinds of games (hi Mom)! I didn't need Sam to tell me that, in Monopoly, the laws of probability mean plenty of chances to land in Jail, but his tips on the next most-likely landing spots (I'm not passing on that secret) will definitely come in handy. I once told Sam that beating me might be easy, but he'd never win against a computer. He said I was wrong: artificial intelligence can win games like chess, where the computer can calculate all the possible moves, but human intuition beats the pants off what he calls the "brute force" calculation method!

"Uh, I don't know," Ralph finally said.

"Leave me alone—I've got my own problems!"

"That's not bad! Got any more?" asked Ralph. "I can add them to my act!"

Oh, no. Not the act! Everyone groaned.

"I can show you some mathematical magic tricks, too," offered Sam. "But we'd better go back to the art room for some supplies."

So, in from the garden we went, and while the reporters and teachers and camera crew and kids were filing into the art room, Sam found a postcard, some string, and a pair of scissors. When everyone

Sam's not the only one with bad jokes...

- Two kids played five games of checkers. Each won the same number of games, with no ties. How can this happen? *Answer:* They weren't playing each other.

- What do you get when you divide the circumference of a jack-o'-lantern by its diameter? *Answer:* Pumpkin pi.

- How many times can you subtract 7 from 83, and what is left afterwards? *Answer:* Subtract as many times as you like—it'll always leave 76.

was settled, he held the postcard out to Ralph and asked, "Think I can walk through this postcard?"

"You're kidding," answered Ralph.

Okay, math or no math, I couldn't see any way Sam could fit through that little piece of cardboard. And I could see "no way" written all over Mr. Lake's face. But, I was pretty sure that Sam knew what he was doing. So I kept my mouth shut and watched as Sam folded the postcard in half, short edges together.

"After folding it, cut a straight line from the fold almost to the opposite edge," said Sam. "Careful not to cut all the way through. Then cut a new line next to it, starting from the edge you just reached, and stop close to the fold. Keep going from opposite sides."

He kept at it this way until he reached the other end. We all waited and wondered what he was doing. Finally, he cut through all the joined bits except the two at the ends, opened it up, and dropped it over his head!

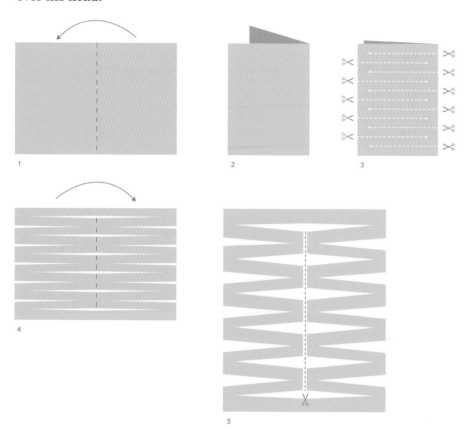

1
2
3
4
5

The kids all hooted their approval. Some of them even applauded. Sam bowed grandly.

"Hey!" sputtered Ralph.

Sam grinned. "Don't be fooled by the amount of space the postcard covers. It might have a small area, but you can actually stretch an incredibly long perimeter out of it!"

"Like fractals: small shapes with infinite perimeter," commented Jen. "It's all geometry."

"Here's another trick," said Sam, taking the two pieces of string, each about two feet long. "I need two volunteers—Mrs. Norton?" The teacher agreed, and Sam tied the ends of the first string around each of her wrists. "Who else?" called Sam. "What about you, Mr. Lake?"

"Me? Uh, um, well…alright, then."

On went the string around Mr. Lake's left wrist. The other end Sam passed under Mrs. Norton's string and looped back to tie around Mr. Lake's right wrist.

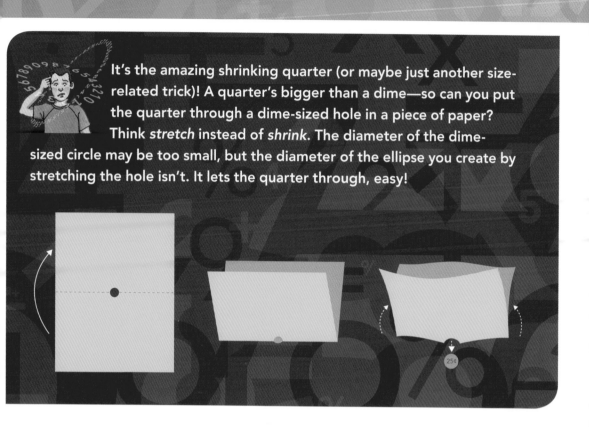

It's the amazing shrinking quarter (or maybe just another size-related trick)! A quarter's bigger than a dime—so can you put the quarter through a dime-sized hole in a piece of paper? Think *stretch* instead of *shrink*. The diameter of the dime-sized circle may be too small, but the diameter of the ellipse you create by stretching the hole isn't. It lets the quarter through, easy!

Sam grinned at the two teachers. "Now try to get out—without untying or cutting the strings."

It sure was funny watching them try. Mr. Lake was starting to sweat and Mrs. Norton was grinding her teeth as they twisted and turned, ducked under, and tried to step over the chain Sam had made with the string and their arms. Finally, Sam showed them how to get free:

"Just take the middle of your string, Mr. Lake, and push it under the string on Mrs. Norton's right wrist, towards her fingers—that's right," explained Sam. "Loop it over her hand, back under the bit on her wrist, and you're free!"

"My act will be *sooo* good!" cried Ralph.

Mr. Lake gave himself a bit of a shake. "Enough of this—we've strayed quite a bit from math now—"

"Actually, we haven't," said Sam. "It was all geometry, the regular sort (you know, Euclidean), plus fractal, topological—name it and you'll find some fun in it."

"What was that last one you said?" I asked. "I can't even pronounce it."

"Topology—let *me* explain," said Ralph.

I looked at him skeptically. "*You* know what topology is?"

"Sure," said Ralph. "The mathematics of making my act top-notch!" He looked around, like he was expecting a laugh. There was none. See what I mean about Ralph? Cor-ny.

"My turn," said Sam. "Topology's the mind-bending kind of stuff I really get excited about." He picked up a pair of scissors and enthusiastically cut out some long strips of paper. "You could call it a twisted take on the kind of geometry we're used to."

"Why would anyone invent a new geometry?" I interrupted. "Like we don't have enough!"

"Mathematicians have to come up with new ideas if old ideas hold them back," answered Sam. "Like when they invented projective geometry to explain perspective in art. Another name for topology is 'rubber sheet geometry.' In plain old Euclidean geometry, things are the same only if everything matches up exactly. Euclidean shapes

Can you tie a knot in a skipping rope without letting go of the ends? Just cross your arms first then pick up an end in each hand. Next, uncross your arms to transfer the knot over to the rope. You won't learn that in Scouts!

are rigid. But it's a completely different story when you're talking topology. You can take a shape like a circle and really deform it— shrink it, stretch it, warp it any way you want it. Even if it ends up looking like a square, you still haven't changed a thing, not unless you've cut, pasted, or punched a hole in it. A topologist will tell you that a circle's equal to a square, a bowl's the same as a plate..."

"...and there's no difference between a donut and a mug, or a mug and a needle. All because you can stretch one into the other, and they all have one hole," concluded Jen.

"Right. And a topologist will tell you that a strip of paper like this has just one side." While he was talking, Sam had given one of his strips of paper a half-twist and taped the ends together. He handed the loop of paper to Ralph.

"Is this another joke?" asked Ralph.

"It's no joke. Draw a line down the middle of this piece of paper and don't take your pen off the paper until you're back at the beginning."

Ralph borrowed a pen and got to work.

"Weird," Ralph cried. "I never took the pen off the paper, which means I stayed on the inside— but then inside became outside and then became inside again. And now that I'm done, the line looks like it's on both sides. It doesn't make sense!"

"It's logical enough if you think about it," said Sam, laughing. "Since you didn't take your pen off the loop to cross over an edge, that means there's just one side. It's called a Möbius strip. Maybe it sounds crazy, but it's real enough to use. Many conveyer belts have a Möbius twist so both sides wear out evenly, and continuous loop recording tapes are made this way, so they can record twice as much data. Like I said, what's abnormal to us is perfectly normal to topologists. Surfaces, and inside and outside regions, and the way they're connected—that's what topologists look at."

"But why?" I asked.

"I'll tell you in a minute. Now try cutting along that line you drew, Ralph. Don't cut in from the side; just snip a hole and cut straight along the line." Sam handed Ralph the scissors.

"Jeremy, topology gives mathematicians new ways to think about problems—like what if the universe isn't infinite, and is connected in-

stead so that it just wraps around with no edges or boundaries, like a Möbius strip? Or, what's the best way to connect things like electrical circuits, computer networks, cell phone connections, or subway lines? Or even, how do you simplify a maze so the way out is clear?"

"Yes, paper is the way to go," said Ralph, who probably wasn't even listening. He was too busy cutting. "Definitely. Paper tricks will be great for my act. Look, the Amazing Ralph will cut this Möbius strip and *presto*! Wait a minute...one twisted loop?"

Queen Victoria liked the book *Alice's Adventures in Wonderland* so much, she wanted to read more works by the same author. Surprise—most of his books were math books! Lewis Carroll, author of *Alice*, was actually a mathematician named Charles Lutwidge Dodgson.

Talk about a split personality! The shy, stuttering mathematician did some seriously studious stuff—lectured on logic and calculus at Oxford University in England, and wrote books with titles like *Condensation of Determinants*. As a children's author, he seemed the complete opposite—he wasn't shy around children, and wrote nonsense poems, stories, and fairy letters (sometimes in looking-glass writing).

Deep down, his personalities weren't really as different as they seemed. The common thread? Mathematics! He liked folding origami shapes and playing with tangrams (pictures made using only seven shapes cut from a square). He invented word puzzles, math and logic puzzles, and games such as an arithmetical version of croquet and circular billiards, which is played on a round table with no pockets. Even his children's books are full of math—*Alice* has lots of logic and *Through the Looking Glass* includes riddles like: "Divide a loaf by a knife. What's the answer to that?"

"That's topology for you." Sam handed Ralph another loop, with three half-twists this time. "Now cut this one."

"That's so tangled," Ralph protested. "I'll get a knot!"

"Nothing wrong with knots," said Sam. "Looking at and unraveling messy mathematical knots can help scientists explain a lot, including how DNA winds and unwinds, and maybe even how the universe works…"

"Hey, was I right, or what?" Ralph interrupted, holding up the loop he had cut, which was now a knot.

"So you like these tricks?" asked Sam.

"Sure," answered Ralph. "What's *knot* to like?"

Almost everyone groaned, even Sam. But not Mr. Lake.

"Fun and games is fine for some folks," said Mr. Lake, obviously looking for more reasons to back up his ban. "But math isn't just fun and games and those Fibi-fractal-phi things. It's full of all those complicated calculations and numbers—far too many numbers."

Can't have knots without string. Scientists are seriously thinking that "superstring theory" might explain it all. This Theory of Everything (I'm not kidding about the name) says the universe is made of tiny, one-dimensional strings vibrating in a 10- or 11-dimensional world. I know 1-D is a line, 2-D is a square, 3-D is a cube, 4-D is a hypercube… but what does a 10-D world look like?

That's when a reporter spoke up. "Mr. Lake," she said, "Clearly, you are not convinced. However, I'd like an opinion from the kids."

All of a sudden she turned to me. "You weren't too upset with the math ban. What do you think now?" she demanded.

What could I say? Sam was my friend—and he did show us a lot of cool stuff—but something was holding me back.

"M e?" I was trying to stall as long as possible. Most of this stuff did seem pretty interesting and I wanted to help Sam, but let's face it—I didn't want to be the only one on his side. Something was still bothering me, though. "I guess this stuff is pretty cool, but…numbers themselves *are* kind of boring," I finished. Did I just agree with Lake? Lame! That's what I was, lame!

It didn't help that other kids nodded. "You're so right," exclaimed Natasha, who was in our grade. "Numbers are so blah. 1, 2, 3, 4…1 + 1 = 2, 2 x 3 = 6. No surprises, no mystery."

No surprises here, either. Natasha's so into mystery novels, it's like she believes she's in one. She's always looking for ulterior motives and asking nosy questions. Had to agree with her, though.

Sam looked really surprised, and a bit frustrated. "Boring?" he said, his voice rising. "No mystery? What about numbers like prime numbers?"

"Just as b-o-r-i-n-g. What's so interesting about them? 'A prime number is a whole number bigger than one that can't be divided without a remainder by any number except itself and one.'" Natasha rattled off the definition we all had to memorize last year.

"They're interesting enough to be worth money," retorted Sam. That got our attention.

"How?" asked Natasha.

"It's no big deal to find small prime numbers. You just use the 'Sieve of Erasthosthenes'—" said Sam.

"Huh?" I asked. That didn't sound easy at all.

"Okay, hard to say, simple to use." Sam continued. "You write out all the numbers starting from 2—because one is definitely not a prime number—up to 100. Skipping 2 and 3, you cross out any other multiples of 2 and 3, 5 and 7." Sam scribbled these out.

	2	3	4	5	6	7	8	9	10
11	12	13	14	15	16	17	18	19	20
21	22	23	24	25	26	27	28	29	30
31	32	33	34	35	36	37	38	39	40
41	42	43	44	45	46	47	48	49	50
51	52	53	54	55	56	57	58	59	60
61	62	63	64	65	66	67	68	69	70
71	72	73	74	75	76	77	78	79	80
81	82	83	84	85	86	87	88	89	90
91	92	93	94	95	96	97	98	99	100

"The rest of the numbers are primes. But apart from that method, mathematicians can't find any pattern for finding primes—which means there is no easy way to tell if a number like 586,156,487,341 is a prime number. You have to make sure that nothing divides into it except one and itself."

"Uh, that could take a while," I said.

"It does, even with computers," said Sam. "That's why $100,000 is waiting for the first person to find a prime number with more than ten million digits. It'll happen soon…the biggest right now is 9,808,358 digits long, and that happened in September 2006."

"Well, that's no good to us—the contest will be over soon." Natasha said.

"But there's also $150,000 for the first hundred-million-digit prime, and $250,000 for the first billion-digit prime," replied Sam.

"Nice!" said Ralph. "Who's putting up all that cash?"

"It's a group that wants to see people putting their computers together to solve massive problems," said Sam. "It takes a lot of computers running 24 hours a day to find prime numbers."

"Still…watching a computer go through numbers?" said Natasha. "Kind of obsessive, if you ask me."

"The bigger the prime, the better for making secret codes," said Sam. He was shrewd, tapping into Natasha's fixation with mysteries.

"What do you mean?" asked Natasha, instantly alert.

"If you want to stump Internet hackers or credit card scammers—or even spies—choose two prime numbers at random and multiply them together to start your code. It takes years to crack anything based on huge prime numbers," explained Sam, "because primes will never run out and nobody's ever going to think of the same one you do."

"Now *that's* cool," said Natasha. I agreed. Why didn't they tell us that in class?

"I'm not sure that I like numbers you can't predict," said Rosa, Natasha's younger sister. She was the cautious one. "There's no pattern to them."

"Then you'll like 'Pascal's triangle.'" Sam pulled the flip chart over from beside the teacher's desk. He quickly drew rows and rows of numbers, stacked in a triangle shape. "This," he announced, "is Pascal's triangle—part of it, at least."

```
                              1
                           1     1
                        1     2     1
                     1     3     3     1
                  1     4     6     4     1
               1     5    10    10     5     1
            1     6    15    20    15     6     1
         1     7    21    35    35    21     7     1
      1     8    28    56    70    56    28     8     1
   1     9    36    84   126   126    84    36     9     1
1    10    45   120   210   252   210   120    45    10     1
 1   11    55   165   330   462   462   330   165    55    11    1
1   12    66   220   495   792   924   792   495   220    66    12    1
1   13    78   186   715  1287  1716  1716  1287   715   186    78   13    1
```

"You actually memorized all that?" said Rosa, "You seriously need to get a life."

Ouch! Coming from a younger kid, that had to hurt…but it didn't faze Sam at all.

"I didn't have to memorize anything," he said. "You start with just ones down the sides. Each of the numbers in between come from adding the two numbers just above."

"Does it ever stop?" I asked, staring in disbelief at the huge triangle he had made so far.

"No, but I am—before my hand drops off," replied Sam, making a face and shaking out his arm. "I've got enough rows now to show you some patterns."

"The only pattern I see is a row going 1, 2, 3, 4, etc., right next to the ones on the outsides." Rosa commented. Sam used red to outline the row she found.

"That's just the beginning. Next to that is a sequence called the triangle numbers." Sam switched to green and boxed the triangle numbers.

```
                              1
                          1       1
                       1     2      1
                    1     3     3     1
                 1     4     6     4     1
              1     5    10    10     5     1
           1     6    15    20    15     6     1
        1     7    21    35    35    21     7     1
     1     8    28    56    70    56    28     8     1
  1     9    36    84   126   126    84    36     9     1
 1    10    45   120   210   252   210   120    45    10    1
1    11    55   165   330   462   462   330   165    55    11    1
1   12    66   220   495   792   924   792   495   220    66    12    1
1   13    78   186   715  1287  1716  1716  1287   715   186    78    13    1
```

"Triangles?" challenged Rosa. "What's so triangular about 1, 3, 6, 10...?"

"Not the numbers...but see what happens if I start stacking dots, like this?" said Sam.

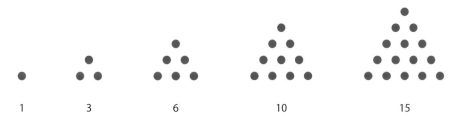

1   3   6   10   15

"That's it? Sure, it's a pattern, but...well, big deal," said Rosa.

"That's not the only pattern," countered Sam. "You know the natural numbers? Start with 1, and just keep adding the next natural number to get the next triangle number. See how that works? 1 is 0 + 1, 3 is 1 + 2, 6 is 1 + 2 + 3, 10 is 1 + 2 + 3 + 4, and so on. And if you add neighboring triangle numbers, you get square numbers—like 1, 4, 9, or 16," he added, drawing dots to make squares.

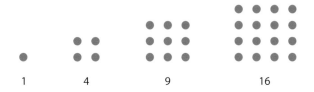

1   4   9   16

Rosa scanned Pascal's triangle with more interest. "Does it have other patterns?"

"Lots of them. Here's one that's not so obvious." Picking up a blue marker, Sam circled some more numbers and printed their totals outside the triangle.

```
                                                                    = 1
                                                                    = 1
                                    1                               = 2
                                                                    = 3
                                 1     1                            = 5
                                                                    = 8
                              1     2     1                         = 13
                                                                    = 21
                           1     3     3     1                      = 34
                        1     4     6     4     1
                     1     5    10    10     5     1
                  1     6    15    20    15     6     1
               1     7    21    35    35    21     7     1
            1     8    28    56    70    56    28     8     1
         1     9    36    84   126   126    84    36     9     1
      1    10    45   120   210   252   210   120    45    10     1
   1    11    55   165   330   462   462   330   165    55    11     1
 1    12    66   220   495   792   924   792   495   220    66    12     1
1    13    78   186   715  1287  1716  1716  1287   715   186    78    13     1
```

"Hey…aren't those Fibonacci numbers?" asked Jen.

"Yup. They really are everywhere, aren't they?" Sam said. "Here's an important pattern for computer programming. Computers read instructions electronically—they only know 'on' as the number 1 and 'off' as the number 0, so they need all info converted into binary numbers, which are numbers written only as 0s and 1s. To get binary numbers, you need to know powers of 2." Sam circled the numbers across each row and wrote the totals at the end, in orange. "Each row of Pascal's triangle gives you one of the powers of two. Add across the rows and you get 1, 2, 4, 8—2^0, 2^1, 2^2, 2^3—and so on."

Parlez-vous binary? Everywhere except in computers, we use a decimal or base-10 system of numbers, so that every position in a number is a power of 10. The number 352 is 3×10^2, plus 5×10^1, plus 2×10^0. Computers speak a language of their own. Each position is a power of 2 instead of 10. So the number 12 in binary is 1,100, or 1×2^3, plus 1×2^2, plus 0×2^1, plus 0×2^0. $8 + 4 + 0 + 0 = 12$.

010001 1100 1, 011 00 1110 1010?

1001 1110 1011... 00 010 1100!

															Power
							1								$1 (2^0)$
						1		1							$2 (2^1)$
					1		2		1						$4 (2^2)$
				1		3		3		1					$8 (2^3)$
			1		4		6		4		1				$16 (2^4)$
		1		5		10		10		5		1			$32 (2^5)$
	1		6		15		20		15		6		1		$64 (2^6)$
1		7		21		35		35		21		7		1	

1   7   21   35   35   21   7   1
1   8   28   56   70   56   28   8   1
1   9   36   84   126   126   84   36   9   1
1   10   45   120   210   252   210   120   45   10   1
1   11   55   165   330   462   462   330   165   55   11   1
1   12   66   220   495   792   924   792   495   220   66   12   1
1   13   78   186   715   1287   1716   1716   1287   715   186   78   13   1

"I get it. Can Pascal patterns help you do any other calculations? What about powers of other numbers?" asked Rosa.

"It doesn't work for all of them," answered Sam enthusiastically. "You can read powers of 11 across rows but it's trickier when you get to double digits and…" Sam stopped in mid-sentence. Rosa was looking nervous again. A little deflated, but unfazed, he continued. "Well, let's try something simpler to start. Have you ever had to add up the numbers to 20?" asked Sam. "We did at my old school."

So we weren't the only ones? Those teachers must share everything. This was one of Mrs. Norton's favorite ways to keep us busy.

"The answer's in Pascal's triangle. Find that diagonal row of natural numbers. Run your finger along that diagonal, and then turn—as if you were drawing a hockey stick. There's your answer: 210. It works every time, no calculator needed," said Sam. "It works for adding the numbers on any diagonal in Pascal's triangle.

"What else can you do?" Rosa asked. She was looking a lot more comfortable, now that we were dealing with predictable numbers. I thought it was pretty cool, myself. Now this was math I could enjoy.

"Pascal's triangle also gives me a fast way to check out my options," continued Sam. "Let's say I have six flavors of jellybeans and I want to try three of them at a time. I'd know in a second that 20 flavor combinations are possible. All I have to do is count down six rows—

the first row is row zero—in the triangle and then slide over to the third number."

```
                          1
                        1   1
                      1   2   1
                    1   3   3   1
                  1   4   6   4   1          1+6+21+56 = 84
                1   5   10  10  5   1
              1   6   15  20  15  6   1
            1   7   21  35  35  21  7   1
          1   8   28  56  70  56  28  8   1
        1   9   36  84  126 126 84  36  9   1
      1   10  45  120 210 252 210 120 45  10  1
    1   11  55  165 330 462 462 330 165 55  11  1
  1   12  66  220 495 792 924 792 495 220 66  12  1
1   13  78  186 715 1287 1716 1716 1287 715 186 78  13  1
```

$$1+7+28+84+210+462+924 = 1716 \qquad 1+12 = 13$$

Srinivasa Ramanujan (1887–1920)

For most mathematicians, life's probably not *all* about numbers. But try telling that to Srinivasa Ramanujan. His obsession started early: he taught himself mathematics from an old book as he grew up in India. Ramanujan went to college on a scholarship, but spent so much time on mathematics, he failed everything else, and could only get work as an accounts clerk. What he really wanted was a job in research—but how could a school dropout like Ramanujan become a researcher?

Desperate, he wrote to English mathematician G.E. Hardy for help. At first, Hardy thought it was a scam. But something about Ramanujan's long, messy list of unproved theorems intrigued Hardy, who ended up inviting Ramanujan to Cambridge University in England to work as a collaborator. Ramanujan almost stayed in India because his beliefs didn't allow travel. In England, Ramanujan suffered from the cold weather. Food shortages brought on by World War I made it hard for the vegetarian mathematician to eat properly, and he often forgot to eat while he worked. But even as Ramanujan grew weaker, his number fixation grew stronger. When a visiting mathematician friend commented that 1729 was a dull number, Ramanujan—tired, frail, and ill in the hospital—fiercely defended 1729 as the smallest number that could be expressed as the sum of two cubes in two different ways. He returned to India and died shortly after, at age 33.

I guess by now I shouldn't be so surprised by the patterns that show up in math—but some of them are so bizarre even I remember them. Like "palindrome numbers"— they read the same backwards and forwards, like 626 or 147,741. You can start with any two-digit number, like 21 and get a palindrome by reversing the digits, 12, and adding them: 21 + 12 = 33. If a palindrome doesn't turn up the first, time, keep it up until you get one: 49 + 94 = 143, not a palindrome, so keep going; 143 + 341 = the palindrome 484. Or perfect numbers—the numbers that add up to a perfect number are also the ones that can be multiplied to make it. Six is a perfect number: 1 + 2 + 3 = 6 and 1 x 2 x 3 = 6. So is 28.

"What did that guy Archimedes say—*eureka*?" I said. "I think I've finally got it. Row six gives you all the options: it says you have one way to eat no jellybeans at all; six ways to try three jellybeans one flavor at a time; 15 ways to pair them up; and 20 ways to have three different beans. If I wanted, I could eat four at a time in 15 different combinations, five at a time in six ways, and only one way to have all six at once." I'd have to buy some jellybeans on the way home—just to practice, of course.

Just then the bell rang. It was the end of the lunch hour. Sam looked at Mr. Lake. So did everyone else. " Well, sir, what do you think now?"

8

You know, for my part, I thought this was a no-brainer. It might have taken me a while to come around, but then, I'm not an easy guy to convince. And I don't think I'm too far off thinking all the kids, even Oscar, were onside now. How could the man not agree?

"This has been a very entertaining hour," said Mr. Lake slowly, "but I'm not changing my mind. The ban stays."

What?!

Mr. Lake turned red and tried to make himself heard over all the kids talking at once. "Math is still too much work, and much too complicated—for you children—no matter how useful it might seem! I have your best interests at heart. You'll thank me one day!" he shouted.

Through all this, Sam stayed quiet. "Well, I guess I haven't convinced you," he said. "Like I promised, I can work for you after school starting today, if you like. But can I have an advance on my first month's pay?"

That was it? Sam was just giving up? I looked around at the teachers for help—Ms. Kay didn't make a move. Neither did the vice principal. We were out of luck. Mr. Lake nodded, with that smirky smile on his face again. Yeah, he was in a good mood now, good enough to agree to anything.

"Thanks, Mr. Lake," Sam replied. "I'll just calculate it out."

So Sam flipped to a new page, and drew this table:

Day	Pay for the Day	Total Pay
1	0.01	0.01
2	0.02	0.03
3	0.04	0.07
4	0.08	0.15
5	0.16	0.31

"No way," exclaimed Ralph. "After five days of work, Sam's going to make only 31 cents? That's not fair."

Sam kept writing.

Day	Pay for the Day	Total Pay
6	0.32	0.63
7	0.64	1.27
8	1.28	2.55
9	2.56	5.11
10	5.12	10.23
11	10.24	20.47
12	20.48	40.95
13	40.96	81.91
14	81.92	163.83
15	163.84	327.67
16	327.68	655.35

"Wicked," said Rosa. "Sam's going to make over $600 by the middle of the month. That's big money."

Mrs. Norton was frowning as she watched the numbers grow. And then I saw it—I could see what he was up to! Genius! And what did mathless Mr. Lake think now? He was getting more and more fidgety with each line.

Day	Pay for the Day	Total Pay
17	655.36	1,310.71
18	1,310.72	2,621.43
19	2,621.44	5,242.87
20	5,242.88	10,485.75
21	10,485.76	20,971.51
22	20,971.52	41,943.03
23	41,943.04	83,886.07
24	83,886.08	167,772.15
25	167,772.16	335,544.31
26	335,544.32	671,088.63
27	671,088.64	1,342,177.27
28	1,342,177.28	2,684,354.55
29	2,684,354.56	5,368,709.11
30	5,368,709.12	10,737,418.23

Mr. Lake's smile was totally gone, and when Sam turned to give him the grand total for the month—$10,737,418.23—the director was sweating like mad.

"I've been thinking it over while you were doing your, er, calculations," said Mr. Lake.

Got him!

"And perhaps I was a bit hasty in making my decision," he continued. Warming up, he went on. "A little hard work doesn't hurt anybody, and math can be useful, no matter what other people say... yes, I've always thought so, underneath it all. I'll admit math isn't my best subject—"

No kidding!

"—so I'd still like you to consider that after-school job, so I'll have a chance to brush up on my math skills." Mr. Lake smiled at Sam. Then he added hastily, "We'd have to negotiate a new wage, of course."

Well, everybody laughed, and the math program stayed on the curriculum. Ms. Kay started a math club, which is pretty popular. Sam, me, Emily, Oscar, Jen, Ralph, Natasha, Rosa, and some other kids joined. Even Mrs. Norton came in to help! You wouldn't believe the stuff we got into: mazes and puzzles, higher dimensions, knot theory, logic and paradoxes, calculus, statistics, game theory, geometries I never even knew existed, and tons more.

We've all got big plans.

Emily's thinking biomechanics. Math will be her secret weapon. She likes how you can mathematically analyze something

like a figure-skating jump or golf swing, and find out exactly what's needed to do it better. Or calculate more energy-efficient or aerodynamic ways to move or position herself to win a race. Plus she can collect data on herself during training and design the ultimate training program so that she works out just enough to improve, but doesn't overdo it. A way to win without working too hard? There's got to be a way for me to use that!

Oscar thinks virtual reality is the way to go—forget just seeing and hearing, he wants the whole experience. He wants to build games with virtual worlds real enough for people to lose themselves in. The way he sees it, his artistic ideas will be so advanced he'll have to master the math himself—no problem for a genius like him. Or he could be a consultant for *The Simpsons*. Sure, they've had producers and writers who were mathematicians before, but hey, with Oscar on board, their ratings will be unbeatable. Whatever, Oscar.

Jen wants to keep her band going. I don't always get her inspiration—she'll convert some mathematical concept like pi into MIDI notes and play them—but what Jen wants, Jen gets. So I won't be surprised to see her topping the charts one day. She also told Oscar to call her up if he ever needed a composer for his games, because she's keen on experimenting with all sorts of digital sound.

Ralph's holding on to his dream: becoming a super-celebrity. I'm not sure about that, but his act *is* better now. His jokes don't stink, and he's not bad at juggling, actually. Maybe studying siteswap notation, which looks at juggling patterns in a mathematical way, helped. He's been thinking about robotics, too, ever since he heard that researchers are working on making a robot that juggles.

Wouldn't it be wild, solving the unsolvable? Ten-year-old Andrew Wiles thought so. He loved math problems and got hooked on the ultimate mystery: "Fermat's Last Theorem." It looked so simple, even he could understand it—but it had remained frustratingly unsolvable for centuries.

Fermat was a 17th-century mathematician who left a mysterious note in the margin of a book. He wrote that the equation $x^n + y^n = z^n$ had no solutions when "n" is bigger than 2. He could prove it, too, he claimed in his note—except the margin was too small for his proof. Fermat died without ever writing down this proof, but mathematicians couldn't resist the challenge: if Fermat could prove it, so could they. So far, they had all been wrong.

Wiles worked on the problem throughout his early teens, but got nowhere. He put the 350-year-old mystery aside

until 1986, when a new, related problem gave him fresh ideas. In 1993 came the sensational news: Andrew Wiles had proved Fermat's Last Theorem, after seven years of secret research. Mathematicians checking his proof found an error, however, and Wiles spent another year immersed in the theorem before inspiration struck again. He repaired his proof and solved the unsolvable. Fermat was right: when "n" is bigger than 2, the equation $x^n + y^n = z^n$ has no solutions.

Rosa dreams about doing something with money. "Yeah, me too," is how I answer her. But seriously, what she really means is doing stock market forecasts or maybe data mining. Data mining? Oh, that's what they call going through the huge amounts of data people collect, looking for patterns and other useful information. Like figuring out buying patterns from the info collected by scanners at the supermarket. Anyway, Rosa likes it when numbers make sense.

Natasha says she wants to be a cryptographer or cryptanalyst, you know, a code-maker or code-breaker. Spy stuff…yeah…I like the sound of that, too. If not, she'll settle for data encryption for companies doing e-commerce, scrambling up credit card information so nobody can steal it out of cyberspace.

Sam and me? Well, Sam said he's wanted to be a physicist since he was five. He wants to answer the big questions: What is time? What does space look like? How did the universe begin? The kind of mind-benders only math can answer.

As for me…I'll be the best friend of the guy who finally settles the Theory-of-Everything question. Other than that, I'm not sure.

Or how about this—one of Ms. Kay's suggestions: she says anything's possible, but thinks I'd make a great math teacher. I'm turning into a pro already, translating for Sam whenever he gets carried away. I can show kids the cool side of math. Like when some new kid starts complaining that math is too hard or that it's only for geniuses or geeks—when that happens, I tell them this story. And you know what they always end up saying?

That's math? Wow—go figure!

Glossary

Algorithm: A set of mathematical rules followed step-by-step to solve a problem.

Arithmetic: The branch of mathematics dealing with calculations such as the addition, subtraction, multiplication, and division of numbers.

Binary: A number system using only 0s and 1s to express numbers. Each number is based on powers of 2 (2^0, 2^1, 2^2, 2^3, 2^4, etc.) in contrast to our normal base-10 counting system, which is based on powers of 10. The number 7 is 111 in binary ($1 \times 2^2 + 1 \times 2^1 + 1 \times 2^0 = 4 + 2 + 1 = 7$).

Biomechanics: Science that analyzes movement in living systems and looks at the forces that act upon them.

Butterfly effect: A famous idea in chaos theory that describes how tiny disturbances can cause dramatic changes in complicated situations over time.

Calculus: The name for two types of mathematics—integral calculus and differential calculus. Integral calculus is one way of computing areas and volumes of complicated shapes. Differential calculus computes values that are always changing, such as how fast you're traveling on a trip where the car's speed keeps changing.

Catenary: A curve created from a heavy cord or chain that hangs between its two ends.

CG (computer generated or computer graphic): Describes an object created using specialized computer software for film or special effects.

CGI (computer generated imagery): Three-dimensional images created using specialized computer software for film or special effects.

Chaos: Describes a situation that's always changing in an irregular way. What happens depends upon fixed rules, but is unpredictable because the situation can change dramatically over a long period of time under the influence of small changes to conditions at the start.

Combination: A selection made from a group of objects when the order of arrangement doesn't matter. *See also* Permutation.

Cryptanalyst: Somebody who deciphers the combination of symbols, letters, or numbers that make up a secret code; a code-breaker.

Cryptographer: Somebody who creates codes by combining symbols, letters, or numbers to hide information; a code-maker.

Data mining: The analysis of large amounts of data to find useful patterns.

Dead reckoning: A method of figuring out the position of a ship or airplane by moving only in straight lines and making sharp turns. The distance traveled between changes of direction can be calculated as long as time, speed, and direction can be measured.

Diameter: The length of any line that cuts a shape such as a circle or ellipse exactly in half. A diameter is twice the radius.

Dimension: A way of talking about the kind of space something takes up. A line has one dimension: length. A square has two dimensions: length and width. A cube has three: length, width, and height. Mathematicians think the universe could have 10 or more dimensions.

Ellipse: The oval shape that results from making a slanted cut through the side of a cone.

Estimate: To carefully guess or give an approximate value based on known information.

Fermat's Last Theorem: A famous mathematical statement that says that no solutions exist for the equation $x^n + y^n = z^n$ if n is bigger than 2 and x, y, z are integers bigger than 0. Named for mathematician Pierre Fermat (1601-1665).

Fibonacci numbers: A sequence of numbers (1, 1, 2, 3, 5, 8, 13, 21, 34...) in which each number is formed by adding the two previous numbers. Named for mathematician Fibonacci (1170-1250).

Fractal: A mathematically constructed, never-ending pattern of shapes that are miniature versions of the whole shape.

Game Theory: A branch of mathematics that analyzes games played for fun and looks at strategy and decision-making in areas such as politics, economics, and the military.

Geodesic dome: A framework of triangles or polygons.

Geometry: A branch of mathematics dealing with objects in space. Euclidean geometry deals with flat and solid (three-dimensional) shapes and is named after the mathematician Euclid (325 BC-265 BC), who laid out the basic theorems and rules of geometry. Non-Euclidean geometries deal with curved space.

Golden ratio: A ratio equal to approximately 1.618... (an irrational number), often appearing in nature. Also known as the golden section or phi.

Golden rectangle: a rectangle that has sides in the ratio 1: 1.618...

Hexagon: A flat figure with six sides and six angles. A regular hexagon has six equal sides and six equal angles.

Hypercube: A four-dimensional object. Also called a tesseract.

Imaginary numbers: Numbers written as real numbers times i, which is the square root of -1 ($\sqrt{-1}$). i was invented to find the square roots of negative numbers, which is logically impossible with real numbers. *See also* Real Numbers.

Infinity (∞): Endlessness. Numbers are infinite, i.e., there is always another number after the biggest number you can think of.

Integers: All whole numbers, whether positive or negative, and zero.

Irrational numbers: Numbers that cannot be completely expressed as a ratio or decimal. They never end and never repeat.

Iteration: The recycling of results back into the same equation or rule.

Knot: A mathematical knot is a closed curve, with no loose ends, in 3-dimensional space.

Logarithmic spiral: An open-ended curve that coils around a given point without changing the angle of the curve. A 3-dimensional spiral is known as a helix.

Metric: The international system of units (abbreviated SI) based on units such as the meter for length and the kilogram for mass.

MIDI (musical instrument digital interface): A standardized method of communication that allows electronic musical instruments and computers to understand the same data.

Möbius strip: A one-sided object in topology that can be modeled by giving a strip of paper a half-twist before taping the ends together.

Motif: The basic unit in a repeated pattern.

Natural numbers: The set of the ordinary counting numbers (1, 2, 3…).

Origami: The art of folding paper.

Palindromes: Numbers, words, or phrases that read the same forwards or backwards. Examples of number palindromes are 121 or 34,743. Word palindromes include "madam" and "radar."

Parabola: The mathematical curve traced by a stream of water from a hose as it shoots up, curves near the top, and heads back down, or the path of a thrown ball.

Paradox: A statement or reasoning that leads to an impossible or obviously wrong solution. An example is Zeno's paradox. Zeno argued that if Achilles gives a tortoise a head start in a race, then Achilles will never catch up. Why? As soon as Achilles reaches the point where the tortoise was, the tortoise will have moved on to another point. The two racers will never be in the same place because the distance, no matter how short, can always be subdivided, and Achilles will always be trying to make up that infinitely small distance. In reality, time can't be divided infinitely, and the sum of infinitely many parts does not total an infinitely large number.

Parallel lines: Lines that will never meet because they are always the same distance apart.

Pascal's triangle: A triangular arrangement of numbers in which every number is the sum of the two numbers above it. The triangle is named after 17th-century French mathematician Blaise Pascal (1623-1662) but was recorded by a Chinese mathematician around 1300 AD and known earlier by Hindu and Arab scholars.

Pattern: A shape, design, or arrangement of numbers (or letters) that repeat in a regular way.

Pentagram: A five-pointed star made by drawing lines from vertex to vertex inside a pentagon and used as a mystic symbol by the Pythagoreans.

Percentage: An amount expressed as a fraction where the denominator is 100.

Perfect number: The numbers that add up to a perfect number are also the ones that can be multiplied to make it. Six is a perfect number: $1 + 2 + 3 = 6$ and $1 \times 2 \times 3 = 6$.

Perimeter: The distance around a closed figure, e.g., a square or pentagon.

Permutation: A selection made from a group of objects, when the order of arrangement matters. *See* Combination.

Perspective: The science of drawing on a two-dimensional surface to create the image of three dimensions.

Phi: *See* Golden ratio.

Pi (π): An irrational number that is the ratio of the circumference of a circle to its diameter. It is usually shown as 3.142, but has been calculated to over a trillion decimal places.

Polygon: A flat, closed shape with straight sides.

Prime numbers: Any number greater than 1 with only two factors—1 and itself.

Probability: A branch of mathematics that uses numbers to predict how likely something is to happen.

Pythagorean Theorem ($a^2+b^2=c^2$): The rule that states that the sum of the squares of two sides of a right-angled triangle is equal to the square of the hypotenuse (the longest side, which is opposite to the right angle).

Radius: The distance between any point on a circle and the centre of that circle.

Random number generator: A device that produces numbers fairly, with no particular order or preference, e.g., dice, spinners, specially designed computer programs.

Ratio: A way of comparing two numbers, e.g., 2:1 (or 2 to 1). Special ratios include pi and the golden ratio.

Rational numbers: Numbers that can be written as a ratio of whole numbers.

Real numbers: All rational and irrational numbers.

Self-similar: Having the same appearance at any magnification.

Sieve of Eratosthenes: A way of finding prime numbers that was invented by the Greek mathematician Eratosthenes (c. 230 BC)

Siteswap notation: A way of writing down juggling patterns.

Square numbers: The product of a number multiplied by itself, e.g., $4 = 2 \times 2$ (or 2 squared or 2^2). Also the number of evenly spaced dots needed to make a square.

Square roots: The number that is multiplied by itself to produce the square number, e.g., 3 is the square root of 9 because $3 \times 3 = 9$.

Statistics: The branch of mathematics that collects, analyzes, and interprets numerical facts.

Tangram: A geometrical puzzle of Chinese origin, consisting of a square cut into seven pieces, which can be combined to create figures and shapes.

Tessellation: An arrangement of shapes that cover an area without gaps or overlaps.

Tetrominoes: Squares joined together along their sides. Five different tetrominoes are possible.

Theory of Everything: A theory that will explain all forces and all matter.

Topology (or rubber-sheet geometry): A branch of mathematics that looks at an object's surfaces, its regions, and connections as the object is bent, squashed, and stretched out of shape without tearing.

Triangle number: 1) A number equal to the sum of all the positive whole numbers before it. Examples include 1, 3, 6, 10, 15, 21.
2) The number of dots needed to make a triangle. The sum of any two consecutive triangle numbers is a square number.

Trigonometry: A branch of mathematics that explores the relations between sides and angles of triangles, especially right-angled triangles.

Vanishing point: The point at which parallel lines leading off into the distance appear to meet.

Whole numbers: Natural numbers and zero (0, 1, 2, 3...).

Further Reading

Non-fiction

G is for Googol: a Math Alphabet Book by David M. Schwartz, illustrated by Marissa Moss (Ten Speed Press, 1998). Covers aspects of mathematics from Abacus to Zillion, stopping in at Googol, Nature and Venn Diagrams along the way. Recommended for grades 3 and up.

Mathematicians Are People Too, Vol. I and *Vol. II* by Luetta and Wilburt Reimer (Dale Seymour Publications, 1990, 1995). Lively stories about famous mathematicians from different times and places and their contributions to the world of mathematics. Recommended for grades 3 to 7.

Math for Smarty Pants by Marilyn Burns, illustrated by Martha Weston (Little, Brown & Co, 1982). A survey of the more-than-bizarre world of numbers, shapes and logic through the eyes of four kids. Suited for grades 4 to 8.

The Brown Paper School Presents: The I Hate Mathematics Book! by Marilyn Burns, illustrated by Martha Weston (Little, Brown & Co, 1975). A skewed tour of the mathematical world, plus puzzles, games and sneaky math tricks for kids. Suited for grades 4 to 8.

Fiction

The Number Devil by Magnus Enzensberger, illustrated by Rotraut Susanne Berner (Henry Holt, 1998). An intriguing story of a young, math-oppressed boy and the irascible Number Devil who appears in his dreams. Suited for kids age 11 and up.

For older readers

The Math Instinct: Why You're a Mathematical Genius (Along with Lobsters, Birds, Cats, and Dogs) by Keith Devlin (Thunder Mouth Press, 2005). A survey of math in nature.

Other media

NUMB3RS

A television series featuring math as a crime-solving tool.

Plus

An online magazine, available at www.plus.maths.org.

Index

About the Authors

Cora Lee combines her love for science and writing by working as a scientific writer for the pharmaceutical and biotechnology industries. She also coordinates the Vancouver chapter of the Canadian Association for Girls in Science and writes science articles for kids. She lives in Vancouver with her family.

Gillian O'Reilly is a freelance writer and editor and is the author of *Slangalicious: Where We Got That Crazy Lingo* (2004). She lives in Toronto with her family.

Virigina Gray is the illustrator of several books for children. She lives in Katoomba, Australia.

Photo Credits